The Grand Duke by Gilbert & Sullivan

or THE STATUTORY DUEL

Libretto by William S. Gilbert
Music by Arthur Sullivan

The partnership between William Schwenck Gilbert and Arthur Seymour Sullivan and their canon of Savoy Operas is rightly lauded by all lovers of comic opera the world over.

Gilbert's sharp, funny words and Sullivan's deliciously lively and hummable tunes create a world that is distinctly British in view but has the world as its audience.

Both men were exceptionally talented and gifted in their own right and wrote much, often with other partners, that still stands the test of time. However, together as a team they created Light or Comic Operas of a standard that have had no rivals equal to their standard, before or since. That's quite an achievement.

To be recognised by the critics is one thing but their commercial success was incredible. The profits were astronomical, allowing for the building of their own purpose built theatre – The Savoy Theatre.

Beginning with the first of their fourteen collaborations, Thespis in 1871 and travelling through many classics including The Sorcerer (1877), H.M.S. Pinafore (1878), The Pirates of Penzance (1879), The Mikado (1885), The Gondoliers (1889) to their finale in 1896 with The Grand Duke, Gilbert & Sullivan created a legacy that is constantly revived and admired in theatres and other media to this very day.

Index of Contents

The Grand Duke, or The Statutory Duel was the final collaboration between Gilbert & Sullivan. It debuted on March 7, 1896 at the Savoy Theatre, London and ran for only 123 performances.

DRAMATIS PERSONAE
RUDOLPH (Grand Duke of Pfennig Halbpfennig).
ERNEST DUMMKOPF (a Theatrical Manager).

LUDWIG (his Leading Comedian).
DR. TANNHUSER (a Notary).
THE PRINCE OF MONTE CARLO.
VISCOUNT MENTONE.
BEN HASHBAZ (a Costumier).
HERALD.

THE PRINCESS OF MONTE CARLO (betrothed to RUDOLPH).
THE BARONESS VON KRAKENFELDT (betrothed to RUDOLPH).
JULIA JELLICOE (an English Comdienne).
LISA (a Soubrette).
Members of Ernest Dummkopf's Company:

OLGA
GRETCHEN
BERTHA
ELSA
MARTHA

Chamberlains, Nobles, Actors, Actresses, etc.

SCENES
ACT I—Scene. Public Square of Speisesaal.
ACT II—Scene. Hall in the Grand Ducal Palace.

DATE - 1750.

MUSICAL NUMBERS
Overture (Includes parts of "The good Grand Duke", "My Lord Grand Duke, farewell!", "With fury indescribable I burn", "Well, you're a pretty kind of fellow", "Strange the views some people hold")
ACT I
1. Won't it be a pretty wedding? (Chorus)
1a. Pretty Lisa, fair and tasty (Lisa and Ludwig with Chorus)
2. By the mystic regulation (Ludwig with Chorus)
3. Were I a king in very truth (Ernest with Chorus)
4. How would I play this part (Julia and Ernest)
5. My goodness me! What shall I do? Ten minutes since I met a chap (Ludwig and Chorus)
6. About a century since (Notary)
7. Strange the views some people hold (Julia, Lisa, Ernest, Notary, and Ludwig)
8. Now take a card and gaily sing (Julia, Lisa, Ernest, Notary, and Ludwig)
9. The good Grand Duke (Chorus of Chamberlains)
9a. A pattern to professors of monarchical autonomy (Grand Duke)
10. As o'er our penny roll we sing (Baroness and Grand Duke)
11. When you find you're a broken-down critter (Grand Duke)

12. Finale, Act I
Come hither, all you people (Ensemble)
Oh, a monarch who boasts intellectual graces (Ludwig with Chorus)
Ah, pity me, my comrades true (Julia with Chorus)
Oh, listen to me, dear (Julia and Lisa with Chorus)
The die is cast (Lisa with Chorus)
For this will be a jolly Court (Ludwig and Chorus)
ACT II
13. As before you we defile (Chorus)
14. Your loyalty our Ducal heart-string touches (Ludwig with Chorus)
14a. At the outset I may mention (Ludwig with Chorus)
15. Yes, Ludwig and his Julia are mated (Ludwig)
15a. Take care of him – he's much too good to live (Lisa)
16. Now Julia, come, consider it from (Julia and Ludwig)
17. Your Highness, there's a party at the door (Chorus)
17a. With fury indescribable I burn (Baroness and Ludwig)
18. Now away to the wedding we go (Baroness and Chorus)
19. So ends my dream, Broken ev'ry promise plighted (Julia)
20. If the light of love's lingering ember (Julia, Ernest, and Chorus)
21. Come, bumpers – aye, ever-so-many (Baroness with Chorus)
22. Why, who is this approaching? (Ludwig and Chorus)
23. The Prince of Monte Carlo (Herald and Chorus)
24. His highness we know not (Ludwig)
25. We're rigged out in magnificent array (Prince of Monte Carlo)
26. Dance
27. Take my advice – when deep in debt (Prince of Monte Carlo with Chorus)
28. Hurrah! Now away to the wedding (Ensemble)
28a.Well, you're a pretty kind of fellow (Grand Duke with Chorus)
29. Happy couples, lightly treading (Ensemble)

ACT I.

SCENE.—Market-place of Speisesaal, in the Grand Duchy of Pfennig Halbpfennig. A well, with decorated ironwork, up L.C. GRETCHEN, BERTHA, OLGA, MARTHA, and other members of ERNEST DUMMKOPF'S theatrical company are discovered, seated at several small tables, enjoying a repast in honour of the nuptials of LUDWIG, his leading comedian, and LISA, his soubrette.

CHORUS
Won't it be a pretty wedding?
Will not Lisa look delightful?
Smiles and tears in plenty shedding—
Which in brides of course is rightful
One could say, if one were spiteful,
Contradiction little dreading,
Her bouquet is simply frightful—
Still, 'twill be a pretty wedding!
Oh, it is a pretty wedding!

Such a pretty, pretty wedding!

LISA
If her dress is badly fitting,
Theirs the fault who made her trousseau.

BERTHA
If her gloves are always splitting,
Cheap kid gloves, we know, will do so.

OLGA
If upon her train she stumbled,
On one's train one's always treading.

GRETCHEN
 If her hair is rather tumbled,
Still, 'twill be a pretty wedding!

CHORUS
Such a pretty, pretty wedding!

CHORUS
Here they come, the couple plighted—
On life's journey gaily start them.
Soon to be for aye united,
Till divorce or death shall part them.

(LUDWIG and LISA come forward.)

DUET—**LUDWIG and LISA**

LUDWIG
Pretty Lisa, fair and tasty,
Tell me now, and tell me truly,
Haven't you been rather hasty?
Haven't you been rash unduly?
Am I quite the dashing sposo
That your fancy could depict you?
Perhaps you think I'm only so-so?
(She expresses admiration.)
Well, I will not contradict you!

CHORUS
No, he will not contradict you!

LISA
 Who am I to raise objection?
I'm a child, untaught and homely—

When you tell me you're perfection,
Tender, truthful, true, and comely—
That in quarrel no one's bolder,
Though dissensions always grieve you—
Why, my love, you're so much older
That, of course, I must believe you!

CHORUS
Yes, of course, she must believe you!

CHORUS
If he ever acts unkindly,
Shut your eyes and love him blindly—
Should he call you names uncomely,
Shut your mouth and love him dumbly—
Should he rate you, rightly—leftly—
Shut your ears and love him deafly.
Ha! ha! ha! ha! ha! ha! ha!
Thus and thus and thus alone
Ludwig's wife may hold her own!

(LUDWIG and LISA sit at table.)

Enter NOTARY TANNHAUSER.

NOTARY TANNHAUSER
Hallo! Surely I'm not late?

(All chatter unintelligibly in reply.)

NOTARY TANNHAUSER
But, dear me, you're all at breakfast! Has the wedding taken place?

(All chatter unintelligibly in reply.)

NOTARY TANNHAUSER
My good girls, one at a time, I beg. Let me understand the situation. As solicitor to the conspiracy to dethrone the Grand Duke—a conspiracy in which the members of this company are deeply involved—I am invited to the marriage of two of its members. I present myself in due course, and I find, not only that the ceremony has taken place—which is not of the least consequence—but the wedding breakfast is half eaten—which is a consideration of the most serious importance.

(LUDWIG and LISA come down.)

LUDWIG
But the ceremony has not taken place. We can't get a parson!

NOTARY TANNHAUSER

Can't get a parson! Why, how's that? They're three a penny!

LUDWIG
Oh, it's the old story—the Grand Duke!

ALL
Ugh!

LUDWIG
It seems that the little imp has selected this, our wedding day, for a convocation of all the clergy in the town to settle the details of his approaching marriage with the enormously wealthy Baroness von Krakenfeldt, and there won't be a parson to be had for love or money until six o'clock this evening!

LISA
And as we produce our magnificent classical revival of Troilus and Cressida to-night at seven, we have no alternative but to eat our wedding breakfast before we've earned it. So sit down, and make the best of it.

GRETCHEN
Oh, I should like to pull his Grand Ducal ears for him, that I should! He's the meanest, the cruellest, the most spiteful little ape in Christendom!

OLGA
Well, we shall soon be freed from his tyranny.
To-morrow the Despot is to be dethroned!

LUDWIG
Hush, rash girl! You know not what you say.

OLGA
Don't be absurd! We're all in it—we're all tiled, here.

LUDWIG
That has nothing to do with it. Know ye not that in alluding to our conspiracy without having first given and received the secret sign, you are violating a fundamental principle of our Association?

SONG—**LUDWIG**
By the mystic regulation
Of our dark Association,
Ere you open conversation
With another kindred soul,
You must eat a sausage-roll!

(Producing one.)

ALL
You must eat a sausage-roll!

LUDWIG

If, in turn, he eats another,
That's a sign that he's a brother—
Each may fully trust the other.
It is quaint and it is droll,
But it's bilious on the whole.

ALL

Very bilious on the whole.

LUDWIG

It's a greasy kind of pasty,
Which, perhaps, a judgement hasty
Might consider rather tasty:
Once (to speak without disguise)
It found favour in our eyes.

ALL

It found favour in our eyes.

LUDWIG

But when you've been six months feeding
(As we have) on this exceeding
Bilious food, it's no ill-breeding
If at these repulsive pies
Our offended gorges rise!

ALL

Our offended gorges rise!

MARTHA

Oh, bother the secret sign! I've eaten it until I'm quite uncomfortable! I've given it six times already to-day—and (whimpering) I can't eat any breakfast!

BERTHA

And it's so unwholesome. Why, we should all be as yellow as frogs if it wasn't for the make-up!

LUDWIG

All this is rank treason to the cause. I suffer as much as any of you. I loathe the repulsive thing—I can't contemplate it without a shudder—but I'm a conscientious conspirator, and if you won't give the sign I will.

(Eats sausage-roll with an effort.)

LISA

Poor martyr! He's always at it, and it's a wonder where he puts it!

NOTARY TANNHAUSER

Well now, about Troilus and Cressida. What do you play?

LUDWIG (struggling with his feelings)
If you'll be so obliging as to wait until I've got rid of this feeling of warm oil at the bottom of my throat, I'll tell you all about it. (LISA gives him some brandy.) Thank you, my love; it's gone. Well, the piece will be produced upon a scale of unexampled magnificence. It is confidently predicted that my appearance as King Agamemnon, in a Louis Quatorze wig, will mark an epoch in the theatrical annals of Pfennig Halbpfennig. I endeavoured to persuade Ernest Dummkopf, our manager, to lend us the classical dresses for our marriage. Think of the effect of a real Athenian wedding procession cavorting through the streets of Speisesaal! Torches burning—cymbals banging—flutes tootling—citharae twanging—and a throng of fifty lovely Spartan virgins capering before us, all down the High Street, singing "Eloia! Eloia! Opoponax, Eloia!" It would have been tremendous!

NOTARY TANNHAUSER
And he declined?

LUDWIG
He did, on the prosaic ground that it might rain, and the ancient Greeks didn't carry umbrellas! If, as is confidently expected, Ernest Dummkopf is elected to succeed the dethroned one, mark any words, he will make a mess of it.

[Exit LUDWIG with LISA.

OLGA
He's sure to be elected. His entire company has promised to plump for him on the understanding that all the places about the Court are filled by members of his troupe, according to professional precedence.

ERNEST enters in great excitement.

BERTHA (looking off).
Here comes Ernest Dummkopf. Now we shall know all about it!

ALL
Well—what's the news? How is the election going?

ERNEST
Oh, it's a certainty—a practical certainty! Two of the candidates have been arrested for debt, and the third is a baby in arms—so, if you keep your promises, and vote solid, I'm cocksure of election!

OLGA
Trust to us. But you remember the conditions?

ERNEST
Yes—all of you shall be provided for, for life. Every man shall be ennobled—every lady shall have unlimited credit at the Court Milliner's, and all salaries shall be paid weekly in advance!

GRETCHEN
Oh, it's quite clear he knows how to rule a Grand Duchy!

ERNEST

Rule a Grand Duchy? Why, my good girl, for ten years past I've ruled a theatrical company! A man who can do that can rule anything!

SONG—**ERNEST**.

Were I a king in very truth,
And had a son—a guileless youth—
In probable succession;
To teach him patience, teach him tact,
How promptly in a fix to act,
He should adopt, in point of fact,
A manager's profession.
To that condition he should stoop
(Despite a too fond mother),
With eight or ten "stars" in his troupe,
All jealous of each other!
Oh, the man who can rule a theatrical crew,
Each member a genius (and some of them two),
And manage to humour them, little and great,
Can govern this tuppenny State!

ALL

Oh, the man, etc.

Both A and B rehearsal slight—
They say they'll be "all right at night"
(They've both to go to school yet);
C in each act must change her dress,
D will attempt to "square the press";
E won't play Romeo unless
His grandmother plays Juliet;
F claims all hoydens as her rights
(She's played them thirty seasons);
And G must show herself in tights
For two convincing reasons—
Two very well-shaped reasons!
Oh, the man who can drive a theatrical team,
With wheelers and leaders in order supreme,
Can govern and rule, with a wave of his fin,
All Europe—with Ireland thrown in!

ALL

Oh, the man, etc.

[Exeunt all but ERNEST.

ERNEST

Elected by my fellow-conspirators to be Grand Duke of Pfennig Halbpfennig as soon as the contemptible little occupant of the historical throne is deposed—here is promotion indeed! Why, instead of playing Troilus of Troy for a month, I shall play Grand Duke of Pfennig Halbpfennig for a lifetime! Yet, am I happy? No—far from happy! The lovely English comdienne—the beautiful Julia, whose dramatic ability is so overwhelming that our audiences forgive even her strong English accent—that rare and radiant being treats my respectful advances with disdain unutterable! And yet, who knows? She is haughty and ambitious, and it may be that the splendid change in my fortunes may work a corresponding change in her feelings towards me!

Enter JULIA JELLICOE.

JULIA
Herr Dummkopf, a word with you, if you please.

ERNEST
Beautiful English maiden—

JULIA
No compliments, I beg. I desire to speak with you on a purely professional matter, so we will, if you please, dispense with allusions to my personal appearance, which can only tend to widen the breach which already exists between us.

ERNEST (aside)
My only hope shattered! The haughty Londoner still despises me! (Aloud.) It shall be as you will.

JULIA
I understand that the conspiracy in which we are all concerned is to develop to-morrow, and that the company is likelyto elect you to the throne on the understanding that the posts about the Court are to be filled by members of your theatricaltroupe, according to their professional importance.

ERNEST
That is so.

JULIA
Then all I can say is that it places me in an extremely awkward position.

ERNEST (very depressed)
I don't see how it concerns you.

JULIA
Why, bless my heart, don't you see that, as your leading lady, I am bound under a serious penalty to play the leading part in all your productions?

ERNEST
Well?

JULIA
Why, of course, the leading part in this production will be the Grand Duchess!

ERNEST
My wife?

JULIA
That is another way of expressing the same idea.

ERNEST (aside—delighted)
I scarcely dared even to hope for this!

JULIA
Of course, as your leading lady, you'll be mean enough to hold me to the terms of my agreement. Oh, that's so like a man! Well, I suppose there's no help for it—I shall have to do it!

ERNEST (aside)
She's mine! (Aloud.) But—do you really think you would care to play that part? (Taking her hand.)

JULIA (withdrawing it)
Care to play it? Certainly not—but what am I to do? Business is business, and I am bound by the terms of my agreement.

ERNEST
It's for a long run, mind—a run that may last many, many years—no understudy—and once embarked upon there's no throwing it up.

JULIA
Oh, we're used to these long runs in England: they are the curse of the stage—but, you see, I've no option.

ERNEST
You think the part of Grand Duchess will be good enough for you?

JULIA
Oh, I think so. It's a very good part in Gerolstein, and oughtn't to be a bad one in Pfennig Halbpfennig. Why, what did you suppose I was going to play?

ERNEST (keeping up a show of reluctance)
But, considering your strong personal dislike to me and your persistent rejection of my repeated offers, won't you find it difficult to throw yourself into the part with all the impassioned enthusiasm that the character seems to demand? Remember, it's a strongly emotional part, involving long and repeated scenes of rapture, tenderness, adoration, devotion—all in luxuriant excess, and all of the most demonstrative description.

JULIA
My good sir, throughout my career I have made it a rule never to allow private feeling to interfere with my professional duties. You may be quite sure that (however distasteful the part may be) if I undertake it, I shall consider myself professionally bound to throw myself into it with all the ardour at my command.

ERNEST (aside—with effusion)
I'm the happiest fellow alive!
(Aloud.) Now—would you have any objection—to—to give me some idea—if it's only a mere sketch—as to how you would play it? It would be really interesting—to me—to know your conception of—of—the part of my wife.

JULIA
How would I play it? Now, let me see—let me see.
(Considering.) Ah, I have it!

BALLAD—**JULIA**
How would I play this part—
The Grand Duke's Bride?
All rancour in my heart
I'd duly hide—
I'd drive it from my recollection
And 'whelm you with a mock affection,
Well calculated to defy detection—
That's how I'd play this part—
The Grand Duke's Bride.

With many a winsome smile
I'd witch and woo;
With gay and girlish guile
I'd frenzy you—
I'd madden you with my caressing,
Like turtle, her first love confessing—
That it was "mock", no mortal would be guessing,
With so much winsome wile
I'd witch and woo!

Did any other maid
With you succeed,
I'd pinch the forward jade—
I would indeed!
With jealous frenzy agitated
(Which would, of course, be simulated),
I'd make her wish she'd never been created—
Did any other maid
With you succeed!

And should there come to me,
Some summers hence,
In all the childish glee
Of innocence,
Fair babes, aglow with beauty vernal,
My heart would bound with joy diurnal!

This sweet display of sympathy maternal,
Well, that would also be
A mere pretence!

My histrionic art
Though you deride,
That's how I'd play that part—
The Grand Duke's Bride!

ENSEMBLE.

ERNEST	JULIA
Oh joy! when two glowing young hearts	My boy, when two glowing young hearts
From the rise of the curtain,	From the rise of the curtain,
Thus throw themselves into their parts	Thus throw themselves into parts,
Success is most certain!	Success is most certain!
If the role you're prepared to endow	The role I'm prepared to endow
With such delicate touches,	With most delicate touches,
By the heaven above us, I vow	By the heaven above us, I vow
You shall be my Grand Duchess!	I will be your Grand Duchess!
(Dance.)	

Enter all the Chorus with LUDWIG, NOTARY, and LISA—all greatly agitated.

EXCITED CHORUS.

My goodness me! What shall we do? Why, what a dreadful situation!
(To LUDWIG) It's all your fault, you booby you—you lump of indiscrimination!
I'm sure I don't know where to go—it's put me into such a tetter—
But this at all events I know—the sooner we are off, the better!

ERNEST
What means this agitato? What d'ye seek?
As your Grand Duke elect I bid you speak!

SONG—**LUDWIG**
Ten minutes since I met a chap
Who bowed an easy salutation—
Thinks I, "This gentleman, mayhap,
Belongs to our Association."
But, on the whole,
Uncertain yet,
A sausage-roll
I took and eat—
That chap replied (I don't embellish)
By eating three with obvious relish.

CHORUS (angrily).

Why, gracious powers,
No chum of ours
Could eat three sausage-rolls with relish!

LUDWIG
Quite reassured, I let him know
Our plot—each incident explaining;
That stranger chuckled much, as though
He thought me highly entertaining.
I told him all,
Both bad and good;
I bade him call—
He said he would:
I added much—the more I muckled,
The more that chuckling chummy chuckled!

ALL (angrily).
A bat could see
He couldn't be
A chum of ours if he chuckled!

LUDWIG
Well, as I bowed to his applause,
Down dropped he with hysteric bellow—
And that seemed right enough, because
I am a devilish funny fellow.
Then suddenly,
As still he squealed,
It flashed on me
That I'd revealed
Our plot, with all details effective,
To Grand Duke Rudolph's own detective!

ALL
What folly fell,
To go and tell
Our plot to any one's detective!

CHORUS
(Attacking LUDWIG.) You booby dense—
You oaf immense,
With no pretence
To common sense!
A stupid muff
Who's made of stuff
Not worth a puff
Of candle-snuff!

Pack up at once and off we go, unless we're anxious to exhibit
Our fairy forms all in a row, strung up upon the Castle gibbet!

[Exeunt Chorus. Manent LUDWIG, LISA, ERNEST, JULIA, and NOTARY.

JULIA
Well, a nice mess you've got us into! There's an end of our precious plot! All up—pop—fizzle—bang—done for!

LUDWIG
Yes, but—ha! ha!—fancy my choosing the Grand Duke's private detective, of all men, to make a confidant of! When you come to think of it, it's really devilish funny!

ERNEST (angrily)
When you come to think of it, it's extremely injudicious to admit into a conspiracy every pudding-headed baboon who presents himself!

LUDWIG
Yes—I should never do that. If I were chairman of this gang, I should hesitate to enrol any baboon who couldn't produce satisfactory credentials from his last Zoological Gardens.

LISA
Ludwig is far from being a baboon. Poor boy, he could not help giving us away—it's his trusting nature—he was deceived.

JULIA (furiously)
His trusting nature! (To LUDWIG.) Oh, I should like to talk to you in my own language for five minutes—only five minutes! I know some good, strong, energetic English remarks that would shrivel your trusting nature into raisins—only you wouldn't understand them!

LUDWIG
Here we perceive one of the disadvantages of a neglected education!

ERNEST (to JULIA)
And I suppose you'll never be my Grand Duchess now!

JULIA
Grand Duchess? My good friend, if you don't produce the piece how can I play the part?

ERNEST
True. (To LUDWIG.) You see what you've done.

LUDWIG
But, my dear sir, you don't seem to understand that the man ate three sausage-rolls. Keep that fact steadily before you. Three large sausage-rolls.

JULIA
Bah!—Lots of people eat sausage-rolls who are not conspirators.

LUDWIG

Then they shouldn't. It's bad form. It's not the game. When one of the Human Family proposes to eat a sausage-roll, it is his duty to ask himself, "Am I a conspirator?" And if, on examination, he finds that he is not a conspirator, he is bound in honour to select some other form of refreshment.

LISA

Of course he is. One should always play the game.

(To NOTARY, who has been smiling placidly through this.)

What are you grinning at, you greedy old man?

NOTARY TANNHAUSER

Nothing—don't mind me. It is always amusing to the legal mind to see a parcel of laymen bothering themselves about a matter which to a trained lawyer presents no difficulty whatever.

ALL

No difficulty!

NOTARY TANNHAUSER

None whatever! The way out of it is quite simple.

ALL

Simple?

NOTARY TANNHAUSER

Certainly! Now attend. In the first place, you two men fight a Statutory Duel.

ERNEST

A Statutory Duel?

JULIA.

A Stat-tat-tatutory Duel! Ach! what a crack-jaw language this German is!

LUDWIG

Never heard of such a thing.

NOTARY TANNHAUSER

It is true that the practice has fallen into abeyance through disuse. But all the laws of Pfennig Halbpfennig run for a hundred years, when they die a natural death, unless, in the meantime, they have been revived for another century. The Act that institutes the Statutory Duel was passed a hundred years ago, and as it has never been revived, it expires to-morrow. So you're just in time.

JULIA

But what is the use of talking to us about Statutory Duels when we none of us know what a Statutory Duel is?

NOTARY TANNHAUSER

Don't you? Then I'll explain.

SONG—**NOTARY**

About a century since,
The code of the duello
To sudden death
For want of breath
Sent many a strapping fellow.
The then presiding Prince
(Who useless bloodshed hated),
He passed an Act,
Short and compact,
Which may be briefly stated.
Unlike the complicated laws
A Parliamentary draftsman draws,
It may be briefly stated.

ALL

We know that complicated laws,
Such as a legal draftsman draws,
Cannot be briefly stated.

NOTARY TANNHAUSER

By this ingenious law,
If any two shall quarrel,
They may not fight
With falchions bright
(Which seemed to him immoral);
But each a card shall draw,
And he who draws the lowest
Shall (so 'twas said)
Be thenceforth dead—
In fact, a legal "ghoest"
(When exigence of rhyme compels,
Orthography forgoes her spells,
And "ghost" is written "ghoest").

ALL (aside)

With what an emphasis he dwells
Upon "orthography" and "spells"!
That kind of fun's the lowest.

NOTARY TANNHAUSER

When off the loser's popped
(By pleasing legal fiction),
And friend and foe
Have wept their woe

In counterfeit affliction,
The winner must adopt
The loser's poor relations—
Discharge his debts,
Pay all his bets,
And take his obligations.

In short, to briefly sum the case,
The winner takes the loser's place,
With all its obligations.

ALL
How neatly lawyers state a case!
The winner takes the loser's place,
With all its obligations!

LUDWIG
I see. The man who draws the lowest card—

NOTARY TANNHAUSER
Dies, ipso facto, a social death. He loses all his civil rights—his identity disappears—the Revising Barrister expunges his name from the list of voters, and the winner takes his place, whatever it may be, discharges all his functions, and adopts all his responsibilities.

ERNEST
This is all very well, as far as it goes, but it only protects one of us. What's to become of the survivor?

LUDWIG
Yes, that's an interesting point, because I might be the survivor.

NOTARY TANNHAUSER
The survivor goes at once to the Grand Duke, and, in a burst of remorse, denounces the dead man as the moving spirit of the plot. He is accepted as King's evidence, and, as a matter of course, receives a free pardon. To-morrow, when the law expires, the dead man will, ipso facto, come to life again—the Revising Barrister will restore his name to the list of voters, and he will resume all his obligations as though nothing unusual had happened.

JULIA.
When he will be at once arrested, tried, and executed on the evidence of the informer! Candidly, my friend, I don't think much of your plot!

NOTARY TANNHAUSER
Dear, dear, dear, the ignorance of the laity! My good young lady, it is a beautiful maxim of our glorious Constitution that a man can only die once. Death expunges crime, and when he comes to life again, it will be with a clean slate.

ERNEST
It's really very ingenious.

LUDWIG (to NOTARY)
My dear sir, we owe you our lives!

LISA (aside to LUDWIG)
May I kiss him?

LUDWIG
Certainly not: you're a big girl now. (To ERNEST) Well, miscreant, are you prepared to meet me on the field of honour?

ERNEST
At once. By Jove, what a couple of fire-eaters we are!

LISA.
Ludwig doesn't know what fear is.

LUDWIG
Oh, I don't mind this sort of duel!

ERNEST
It's not like a duel with swords. I hate a duel with swords. It's not the blade I mind—it's the blood.

LUDWIG
And I hate a duel with pistols. It's not the ball I mind—it's the bang.

NOTARY TANNHAUSER
Altogether it is a great improvement on the old method of giving satisfaction.

QUINTET - **LUDWIG, LISA, NOTARY, ERNEST, JULIA.**
Strange the views some people hold!
Two young fellows quarrel—
Then they fight, for both are bold—
Rage of both is uncontrolled—
Both are stretched out, stark and cold!
Prithee, where's the moral?
Ding dong! Ding dong!
There's an end to further action,
And this barbarous transaction
Is described as "satisfaction"!
Ha! ha! ha! ha! satisfaction!
Ding dong! Ding dong!
Each is laid in churchyard mould—
Strange the views some people hold!

Better than the method old,
Which was coarse and cruel,
Is the plan that we've extolled.

Sing thy virtues manifold
(Better than refined gold),
Statutory Duel!
Sing song! Sing song!

Sword or pistol neither uses—
Playing card he lightly chooses,
And the loser simply loses!
Ha! ha! ha! ha! simply loses.
Sing song! Sing song!
Some prefer the churchyard mould!
Strange the views some people hold!

NOTARY TANNHAUSER (offering a card to ERNEST).
Now take a card and gaily sing
How little you care for Fortune's rubs—

ERNEST (drawing a card).
Hurrah, hurrah!—I've drawn a King:

ALL
He's drawn a King!
He's drawn a King!
Sing Hearts and Diamonds, Spades and Clubs!

ALL (dancing).
He's drawn a King!
How strange a thing!
An excellent card—his chance it aids—
Sing Hearts and Diamonds, Spades and Clubs—
Sing Diamonds, Hearts and Clubs and Spades!

NOTARY TANNHAUSER (to LUDWIG).
Now take a card with heart of grace—
(Whatever our fate, let's play our parts).

LUDWIG (drawing card).
Hurrah, hurrah!—I've drawn an Ace!

ALL
He's drawn an Ace!
He's drawn an Ace!
Sing Clubs and Diamonds, Spades and Hearts!

ALL (dancing).
He's drawn an Ace!
Observe his face—
Such very good fortune falls to few—

Sing Clubs and Diamonds, Spades and Hearts—
Sing Clubs, Spades, Hearts and Diamonds too!

NOTARY TANNHAUSER
That both these maids may keep their troth,
And never misfortune them befall,
I'll hold 'em as trustee for both—

ALL
He'll hold 'em both!
He'll hold 'em both!
Sing Hearts, Clubs, Diamonds, Spades and all!

ALL (dancing).
By joint decree
As our/your trustee
This Notary we/you will now instal—
In custody let him keep their/our hearts,
Sing Hearts, Clubs, Diamonds, Spades and all!

[Dance and exeunt LUDWIG, ERNEST, and NOTARY with the two Girls.

March. Enter the seven CHAMBERLAINS of the GRAND DUKE RUDOLPH.

CHORUS OF CHAMBERLAINS
The good Grand Duke of Pfennig Halbpfennig,
Though, in his own opinion, very very big,
In point of fact he's nothing but a miserable prig
Is the good Grand Duke of Pfennig Halbpfennig!

Though quite contemptible, as every one agrees,
We must dissemble if we want our bread and cheese,
So hail him in a chorus, with enthusiasm big,
The good Grand Duke of Pfennig Halbpfennig!

Enter the GRAND DUKE RUDOLPH. He is meanly and miserably dressed in old and patched clothes, but blazes with a profusion of orders and decorations. He is very weak and ill, from low living.

SONG—**RUDOLPH**.
A pattern to professors of monarchical autonomy,
I don't indulge in levity or compromising bonhomie,
But dignified formality, consistent with economy,
Above all other virtues I particularly prize.
I never join in merriment—I don't see joke or jape any—
I never tolerate familiarity in shape any—
This, joined with an extravagant respect for tuppence-ha'penny,
A keynote to my character sufficiently supplies.

(Speaking.) Observe. (To CHAMBERLAINS) My snuff-box!

(The snuff-box is passed with much ceremony from the Junior CHAMBERLAIN, through all the others, until it is presented by the Senior CHAMBERLAIN to RUDOLPH, who uses it.)

That incident a keynote to my character supplies.

RUDOLPH
I weigh out tea and sugar with precision mathematical—
Instead of beer, a penny each—my orders are emphatical—
(Extravagance unpardonable, any more than that I call),
But, on the other hand, my Ducal dignity to keep—
All Courtly ceremonial—to put it comprehensively—
I rigidly insist upon (but not, I hope, offensively)
Whenever ceremonial can be practised inexpensively—
And, when you come to think of it, it's really very cheap!

(Speaking.) Observe. (To CHAMBERLAINS) My handkerchief!

(Handkerchief is handed by Junior CHAMBERLAIN to the next in order, and so on until it reaches RUDOLPH, who is much inconvenienced by the delay.)

It's sometimes inconvenient, but it's always very cheap!

RUDOLPH
My Lord Chamberlain, as you are aware, my marriage with the wealthy Baroness von Krakenfeldt will take place to-morrow, and you will be good enough to see that the rejoicings are on a scale of unusual liberality. Pass that on. (Chamberlain whispers to Vice-Chamberlain, who whispers to the next, and so on.) The sports will begin with a Wedding Breakfast Bee. The leading pastry-cooks of the town will be invited to compete, and the winner will not only enjoy the satisfaction of seeing his breakfast devoured by the Grand Ducal pair, but he will also be entitled to have the Arms of Pfennig Halbpfennig tattoo'd between his shoulder-blades. The Vice-Chamberlain will see to this. All the public fountains of Speisesaal will run with Gingerbierheim and Currantweinmilch at the public expense. The Assistant Vice-Chamberlain will see to this. At night, everybody will illuminate; and as I have no desire to tax the public funds unduly, this will be done at the inhabitants' private expense. The Deputy Assistant Vice-Chamberlain will see to this. All my Grand Ducal subjects will wear new clothes, and the Sub-Deputy Assistant Vice-Chamberlain will collect the usual commission on all sales. Wedding presents (which, on this occasion, should be on a scale of extraordinary magnificence) will be received at the Palace at any hour of the twenty-four, and the Temporary Sub-Deputy Assistant Vice-Chamberlain will sit up all night for this purpose. The entire population will be commanded to enjoy themselves, and with this view the Acting Temporary Sub-Deputy Assistant Vice-Chamberlain will sing comic songs in the Market-place from noon to nightfall. Finally, we have composed a Wedding Anthem, with which the entire population are required to provide themselves. It can be obtained from our Grand Ducal publishers at the usual discount price, and all the Chamberlains will be expected to push the sale.

(CHAMBERLAINS bow and exeunt)

I don't feel at all comfortable. I hope I'm not doing a foolish thing in getting married. After all, it's a poor heart that never rejoices, and this wedding of mine is the first little treat I've allowed myself since my christening. Besides, Caroline's income is very considerable, and as her ideas of economy are quite on a par with mine, it ought to turn out well. Bless her tough old heart, she's a mean little darling! Oh, here she is, punctual to her appointment!

Enter BARONESS VON KRAKENFELDT.

BARONESS VON KRAKENFELDT
Rudolph! Why, what's the matter?

RUDOLPH
Why, I'm not quite myself, my pet. I'm a little worried and upset. I want a tonic. It's the low diet, I think. I am afraid, after all, I shall have to take the bull by the horns and have an egg with my breakfast.

BARONESS VON KRAKENFELDT
I shouldn't do anything rash, dear. Begin with a jujube.

(Gives him one.)

RUDOLPH (about to eat it, but changes his mind)
I'll keep it for supper.

(He sits by her and tries to put his arm round her waist.)

BARONESS VON KRAKENFELDT
Rudolph, don't! What in the world are you thinking of?

RUDOLPH
I was thinking of embracing you, my sugarplum. Just as a little cheap treat.

BARONESS VON KRAKENFELDT
What, here? In public? Really, you appear to have no sense of delicacy.

RUDOLPH
No sense of delicacy, Bon-bon!

BARONESS VON KRAKENFELDT
No. I can't make you out. When you courted me, all your courting was done publicly in the Marketplace. When you proposed to me, you proposed in the Market-place. And now that we're engaged you seem to desire that our first tete-a-tete occur in the Marketplace!
Surely you've a room in your Palace—with blinds—that would do?

RUDOLPH
But, my own, I can't help myself. I'm bound by my own decree.

BARONESS VON KRAKENFELDT
Your own decree?

RUDOLPH

Yes. You see, all the houses that give on the Market-place belong to me, but the drains (which date back to the reign of Charlemagne) want attending to, and the houses wouldn't let—so, with a view to increasing the value of the property, I decreed that all love-episodes between affectionate couples should take place, in public, on this spot, every Monday, Wednesday, and Friday, when the band doesn't play.

BARONESS VON KRAKENFELDT

Bless me, what a happy idea! So moral too! And have you found it answer?

RUDOLPH

Answer? The rents have gone up fifty per cent, and the sale of opera-glasses (which is a Grand Ducal monopoly) has received an extraordinary stimulus! So, under the circumstances, would you allow me to put my arm round your waist? As a source of income. Just once!

BARONESS VON KRAKENFELDT

But it's so very embarrassing. Think of the opera-glasses!

RUDOLPH

My good girl, that's just what I am thinking of. Hang it all, we must give them something for their money! What's that?

BARONESS VON KRAKENFELDT (unfolding paper, which contains a large letter, which she hands to him). It's a letter which your detective asked me to hand to you. I wrapped it up in yesterday's paper to keep it clean.

RUDOLPH

Oh, it's only his report! That'll keep. But, I say, you've never been and bought a newspaper?

BARONESS VON KRAKENFELDT

My dear Rudolph, do you think I'm mad? It came wrapped round my breakfast.

RUDOLPH (relieved)

I thought you were not the sort of girl to go and buy a newspaper! Well, as we've got it, we may as well read it. What does it say?

BARONESS VON KRAKENFELDT

Why—dear me—here's your biography! "Our Detested Despot!"

RUDOLPH

Yes—I fancy that refers to me.

BARONESS VON KRAKENFELDT

And it says—Oh, it can't be!

RUDOLPH

What can't be?

BARONESS VON KRAKENFELDT

Why, it says that although you're going to marry me to-morrow, you were betrothed in infancy to the Princess of Monte Carlo!

RUDOLPH

Oh yes—that's quite right. Didn't I mention it?

BARONESS VON KRAKENFELDT

Mention it! You never said a word about it!

RUDOLPH

Well, it doesn't matter, because, you see, it's practically off.

BARONESS VON KRAKENFELDT

Practically off?

RUDOLPH

Yes. By the terms of the contract the betrothal is void unless the Princess marries before she is of age. Now, her father, the Prince, is stony-broke, and hasn't left his house for years for fear of arrest. Over and over again he has implored me to come to him to be married-but in vain. Over and over again he has implored me to advance him the money to enable the Princess to come to me—but in vain. I am very young, but not as young as that; and as the Princess comes of age at two tomorrow, why at two to-morrow I'm a free man, so I appointed that hour for our wedding, as I shall like to have as much marriage as I can get for my money.

BARONESS VON KRAKENFELDT

I see. Of course, if the married state is a happy state, it's a pity to waste any of it.

RUDOLPH

Why, every hour we delayed I should lose a lot of you and you'd lose a lot of me!

BARONESS VON KRAKENFELDT

My thoughtful darling! Oh, Rudolph, we ought to be very happy!

RUDOLPH

If I'm not, it'll be my first bad investment. Still, there is such a thing as a slump even in Matrimonials.

BARONESS VON KRAKENFELDT

I often picture us in the long, cold, dark December evenings, sitting close to each other and singing impassioned duets to keep us warm, and thinking of all the lovely things we could afford to buy if we chose, and, at the same time, planning out our lives in a spirit of the most rigid and exacting economy!

RUDOLPH

It's a most beautiful and touching picture of connubial bliss in its highest and most rarefied development!

DUET—**BARONESS and RUDOLPH**

BARONESS VON KRAKENFELDT
As o'er our penny roll we sing,
It is not reprehensive
To think what joys our wealth would bring
Were we disposed to do the thing
Upon a scale extensive.
There's rich mock-turtle—thick and clear—

RUDOLPH (confidentially)
Perhaps we'll have it once a year!

BARONESS VON KRAKENFELDT (delighted).
You are an open-handed dear!

RUDOLPH
Though, mind you, it's expensive.

BARONESS VON KRAKENFELDT
No doubt it is expensive.

BOTH
How fleeting are the glutton's joys!
With fish and fowl he lightly toys,

RUDOLPH
And pays for such expensive tricks
Sometimes as much as two-and-six!

BARONESS VON KRAKENFELDT
As two-and-six?

RUDOLPH
As two-and-six—

BOTH
Sometimes as much as two-and-six!

BARONESS VON KRAKENFELDT
It gives him no advantage, mind—
For you and he have only dined,
And you remain when once it's down
A better man by half-a-crown.

RUDOLPH
By half-a-crown?

BARONESS VON KRAKENFELDT

By half-a-crown.

BOTH
Yes, two-and-six is half-a-crown.
Then let us be modestly merry,
And rejoice with a derry down derry.
For to laugh and to sing
No extravagance bring—
It's a joy economical, very!

BARONESS VON KRAKENFELDT
Although as you're of course aware
(I never tried to hide it)
I moisten my insipid fare
With water—which I can't abear—

RUDOLPH
Nor I—I can't abide it.

BARONESS VON KRAKENFELDT
This pleasing fact our souls will cheer,
With fifty thousand pounds a year
We could indulge in table beer!

RUDOLPH
Get out!

BARONESS VON KRAKENFELDT
We could—I've tried it!

RUDOLPH
Yes, yes, of course you've tried it!

BOTH
Oh, he who has an income clear
Of fifty thousand pounds a year—

BARONESS VON KRAKENFELDT
Can purchase all his fancy loves
Conspicuous hats—

RUDOLPH
Two shilling gloves—

BARONESS VON KRAKENFELDT (doubtfully)
Two-shilling gloves?

RUDOLPH (positively)

Two-shilling gloves—

BOTH
Yes, think of that, two-shilling gloves!

BARONESS VON KRAKENFELDT
Cheap shoes and ties of gaudy hue,
And Waterbury watches, too—
And think that he could buy the lot
Were he a donkey—

RUDOLPH
Which he's not!

BARONESS VON KRAKENFELDT
Oh no, he's not!

RUDOLPH
Oh no, he's not!

BOTH (dancing).
That kind of donkey he is not!
Then let us be modestly merry,
And rejoice with a derry down derry.
For to laugh and to sing
Is a rational thing-
It's a joy economical, very!

[Exit BARONESS.

RUDOLPH
Oh, now for my detective's report. (Opens letter.)
What's this! Another conspiracy! A conspiracy to depose me!
And my private detective was so convulsed with laughter at the notion of a conspirator selecting him for a confidant that he was physically unable to arrest the malefactor! Why, it'll come off! This comes of engaging a detective with a keen sense of the ridiculous! For the future I'll employ none but Scotchmen. And the plot is to explode to-morrow! My wedding day! Oh, Caroline, Caroline! (Weeps.) This is perfectly frightful! What's to be done? I don't know! I ought to keep cool and think, but you can't think when your veins are full of hot soda-water, and your brain's fizzing like a firework, and all your faculties are jumbled in a perfect whirlpool of tumblication! And I'm going to be ill! I know I am! I've been living too low, and I'm going to be very ill indeed!

SONG—**RUDOLPH.**
When you find you're a broken-down critter,
Who is all of a trimmle and twitter,
With your palate unpleasantly bitter,
As if you'd just eaten a pill—
When your legs are as thin as dividers,

And you're plagued with unruly insiders,
And your spine is all creepy with spiders,
And you're highly gamboge in the gill—
When you've got a beehive in your head,
And a sewing machine in each ear,
And you feel that you've eaten your bed,
And you've got a bad headache down here—
When such facts are about,
And these symptoms you find
In your body or crown—
Well, you'd better look out,
You may make up your mind
You had better lie down!

When your lips are all smeary—like tallow,
And your tongue is decidedly yellow,
With a pint of warm oil in your swallow,
And a pound of tin-tacks in your chest—
When you're down in the mouth with the vapours,
And all over your Morris wall-papers
Black-beetles are cutting their capers,
And crawly things never at rest—
When you doubt if your head is your own,
And you jump when an open door slams—
Then you've got to a state which is known
To the medical world as "jim-jams"
If such symptoms you find
In your body or head,
They're not easy to quell—
You may make up your mind
You are better in bed,
For you're not at all well!

(Sinks exhausted and weeping at foot of well.)

Enter LUDWIG.

LUDWIG
Now for my confession and full pardon. They told me the Grand Duke was dancing duets in the Market-place, but I don't see him. (Sees RUDOLPH.) Hallo! Who's this? (Aside.) Why, it is the Grand Duke!

RUDOLPH (sobbing)
Who are you, sir, who presume to address me in person? If you've anything to communicate, you must fling yourself at the feet of my Acting Temporary Sub-Deputy Assistant Vice-Chamberlain, who will fling himself at the feet of his immediate superior, and so on, with successive foot-flingings through the various grades—your communication will, in course of time, come to my august knowledge.

LUDWIG

But when I inform your Highness that in me you see the most unhappy, the most unfortunate, the most completely miserable man in your whole dominion—

RUDOLPH (still sobbing)
You the most miserable man in my whole dominion? How can you have the face to stand there and say such a thing? Why, look at me! Look at me!

(Bursts into tears.)

LUDWIG
Well, I wouldn't be a cry-baby.

RUDOLPH
A cry-baby? If you had just been told that you were going to be deposed to-morrow, and perhaps blown up with dynamite for all I know, wouldn't you be a cry-baby? I do declare if I could only hit upon some cheap and painless method of putting an end to an existence which has become insupportable, I would unhesitatingly adopt it!

LUDWIG
You would? (Aside.) I see a magnificent way out of this! By Jupiter, I'll try it! (Aloud.) Are you, by any chance, in earnest?

RUDOLPH
In earnest? Why, look at me!

LUDWIG
If you are really in earnest—if you really desire to escape scot-free from this impending—this unspeakably horrible catastrophe—without trouble, danger, pain, or expense—why not resort to a Statutory Duel?

RUDOLPH
A Statutory Duel?

LUDWIG
Yes. The Act is still in force, but it will expire to-morrow afternoon. You fight—you lose—you are dead for a day. To-morrow, when the Act expires, you will come to life again and resume your Grand Duchy as though nothing had happened. In the meantime, the explosion will have taken place and the survivor will have had to bear the brunt of it.

RUDOLPH
Yes, that's all very well, but who'll be fool enough to be the survivor?

LUDWIG (kneeling)
Actuated by an overwhelming sense of attachment to your Grand Ducal person, I unhesitatingly offer myself as the victim of your subjects' fury.

RUDOLPH

You do? Well, really that's very handsome. I daresay being blown up is not nearly as unpleasant as one would think.

LUDWIG
Oh, yes it is. It mixes one up, awfully!

RUDOLPH
But suppose I were to lose?

LUDWIG
Oh, that's easily arranged. (Producing cards.) I'll put an Ace up my sleeve—you'll put a King up yours. When the drawing takes place, I shall seem to draw the higher card and you the lower. And there you are!

RUDOLPH
Oh, but that's cheating.

LUDWIG
So it is. I never thought of that.

(Going.)

RUDOLPH (hastily).
Not that I mind. But I say—you won't take an unfair advantage of your day of office? You won't go tipping people, or squandering my little savings in fireworks, or any nonsense of that sort?

LUDWIG
I am hurt—really hurt—by the suggestion.

RUDOLPH
You—you wouldn't like to put down a deposit, perhaps?

LUDWIG
No. I don't think I should like to put down a deposit.

RUDOLPH
Or give a guarantee?

LUDWIG
A guarantee would be equally open to objection.

RUDOLPH
It would be more regular. Very well, I suppose you must have your own way.

LUDWIG
Good. I say—we must have a devil of a quarrel!

RUDOLPH

Oh, a devil of a quarrel!

LUDWIG
Just to give colour to the thing. Shall I give you a sound thrashing before all the people? Say the word—it's no trouble.

RUDOLPH
No, I think not, though it would be very convincing and it's extremely good and thoughtful of you to suggest it. Still, a devil of a quarrel!

LUDWIG
Oh, a devil of a quarrel!

RUDOLPH
No half measures. Big words—strong language—rude remarks. Oh, a devil of a quarrel!

LUDWIG
Now the question is, how shall we summon the people?

RUDOLPH
Oh, there's no difficulty about that. Bless your heart, they've been staring at us through those windows for the last half-hour!

FINALE.

RUDOLPH
Come hither, all you people—
When you hear the fearful news,
All the pretty women weep'll,
Men will shiver in their shoes.

LUDWIG
And they'll all cry "Lord, defend us!"
When they learn the fact tremendous
That to give this man his gruel
In a Statutory Duel—

BOTH
This plebeian man of shoddy—
This contemptible nobody—
Your Grand Duke does not refuse!

(During this, CHORUS of men and women have entered, all trembling with apprehension under the impression that they are to be arrested for their complicity in the conspiracy.)

CHORUS
With faltering feet,
And our muscles in a quiver,

Our fate we meet
With our feelings all unstrung!
If our plot complete
He has managed to diskiver,
There is no retreat—
We shall certainly be hung!

RUDOLPH (aside to LUDWIG).
Now you begin and pitch it strong—walk into me abusively—

LUDWIG (aside to RUDOLPH).
I've several epithets that I've reserved for you exclusively.
A choice selection I have here when you are ready to begin.

RUDOLPH
Now you begin

LUDWIG
No, you begin—

RUDOLPH
No, you begin—

LUDWIG
No, you begin!

CHORUS (trembling).
Has it happed as we expected?
Is our little plot detected?

DUET—**RUDOLPH and LUDWIG**

RUDOLPH (furiously)
Big bombs, small bombs, great guns and little ones!
Put him in a pillory!
Rack him with artillery!

LUDWIG (furiously).
Long swords, short swords, tough swords and brittle ones!
Fright him into fits!
Blow him into bits!

RUDOLPH
You muff, sir!

LUDWIG
You lout, sir!

RUDOLPH
Enough, sir!

LUDWIG
Get out, sir!

(Pushes him.)

RUDOLPH
A hit, sir?

LUDWIG
Take that, sir!

(Slaps him.)

RUDOLPH
It's tit, sir,

LUDWIG
For tat, sir!

CHORUS (appalled).
When two doughty heroes thunder,
All the world is lost in wonder;
When such men their temper lose,
Awful are the words they use!

LUDWIG
Tall snobs, small snobs, rich snobs and needy ones!

RUDOLPH (jostling him).
Whom are you alluding to?

LUDWIG (jostling him).
Where are you intruding to?

RUDOLPH
Fat snobs, thin snobs, swell snobs and seedy ones!

LUDWIG
I rather think you err.
To whom do you refer?

RUDOLPH
To you, sir!

LUDWIG

To me, sir?

RUDOLPH
I do, sir!

LUDWIG
We'll see, sir!

RUDOLPH
I jeer, sir!
(Makes a face at LUDWIG.) Grimace, sir!

LUDWIG
Look here, sir—
(Makes a face at RUDOLPH.) A face, sir!

CHORUS (appalled).
When two heroes, once pacific,
Quarrel, the effect's terrific!
What a horrible grimace!
What a paralysing face!

ALL
Big bombs, small bombs, etc.

LUDWIG and RUDOLPH (recit.).
He has insulted me, and, in a breath,
This day we fight a duel to the death!

NOTARY TANNHAUSER (checking them).
You mean, of course, by duel (verbum sat.),
A Statutory Duel.

ALL
Why, what's that?

NOTARY TANNHAUSER
According to established legal uses,
A card apiece each bold disputant chooses—
Dead as a doornail is the dog who loses—
The winner steps into the dead man's shoeses!

ALL
The winner steps into the dead man's shoeses!

RUDOLPH and LUDWIG
Agreed! Agreed!

RUDOLPH
Come, come—the pack!

LUDWIG (producing one).
Behold it here!

RUDOLPH
I'm on the rack!

LUDWIG
I quake with fear!

(NOTARY offers card to LUDWIG.)

LUDWIG
First draw to you!

RUDOLPH
If that's the case,
Behold the King!

(Drawing card from his sleeve.)

LUDWIG (same business).
Behold the Ace!

CHORUS
Hurrah, hurrah! Our Ludwig's won
And wicked Rudolph's course is run—
So Ludwig will as Grand Duke reign
Till Rudolph comes to life again—

RUDOLPH
Which will occur to-morrow!
I come to life to-morrow!

GRETCHEN (with mocking curtsey).
My Lord Grand Duke, farewell!
A pleasant journey, very,
To your convenient cell
In yonder cemetery!

LISA (curtseying).
Though malcontents abuse you,
We're much distressed to lose you!
You were, when you were living,
So liberal, so forgiving!

BERTHA
So merciful, so gentle!
So highly ormamental!

OLGA
And now that you've departed,
You leave us broken-hearted!

ALL (pretending to weep).
Yes, truly, truly, truly, truly—
Truly broken-hearted!
Ha! ha! ha! ha! ha! ha! (Mocking him.)

RUDOLPH (furious).
Rapscallions, in penitential fires,
You'll rue the ribaldry that from you falls!
To-morrow afternoon the law expires.
And then—look out for squalls!

[Exit RUDOLPH, amid general ridicule.

CHORUS
Give thanks, give thanks to wayward fate—
By mystic fortune's sway,
Our Ludwig guides the helm of State
For one delightful day!

(To LUDWIG.)
We hail you, sir!
We greet you, sir!
Regale you, sir!
We treat you, sir!
Our ruler be
By fate's decree
For one delightful day!

NOTARY TANNHAUSER
You've done it neatly! Pity that your powers
Are limited to four-and-twenty hours!

LUDWIG
No matter, though the time will quickly run,
In hours twenty-four much may be done!

SONG—**LUDWIG**
Oh, a Monarch who boasts intellectual graces
Can do, if he likes, a good deal in a day—
He can put all his friends in conspicuous places,

With plenty to eat and with nothing to pay!
You'll tell me, no doubt, with unpleasant grimaces,
To-morrow, deprived of your ribbons and laces,
You'll get your dismissal—with very long faces—
But wait! on that topic I've something to say!
(Dancing.)
I've something to say—I've something to say—I've something to say!
Oh, our rule shall be merry—I'm not an ascetic—
And while the sun shines we will get up our hay—
By a pushing young Monarch, of turn energetic,
A very great deal may be done in a day!

CHORUS
Oh, his rule will be merry, etc.

(During this, LUDWIG whispers to NOTARY, who writes.)

For instance, this measure (his ancestor drew it),
(alluding to NOTARY)
This law against duels—to-morrow will die—
The Duke will revive, and you'll certainly rue it—
He'll give you "what for" and he'll let you know why!
But in twenty-four hours there's time to renew it—
With a century's life I've the right to imbue it—
It's easy to do—and, by Jingo, I'll do it!

(Signing paper, which NOTARY presents.)

It's done! Till I perish your Monarch am I!
Your Monarch am I—your Monarch am I—your Monarch am I!
Though I do not pretend to be very prophetic,
I fancy I know what you're going to say—
By a pushing young Monarch, of turn energetic,
A very great deal may be done in a day!

ALL (astonished).
Oh, it's simply uncanny, his power prophetic—
It's perfectly right—we were going to say,
By a pushing, etc.

Enter JULIA, at back.

LUDWIG (recit.)
This very afternoon—at two (about)—
The Court appointments will be given out.
To each and all (for that was the condition)
According to professional position!

ALL
Hurrah!

JULIA (coming forward).
According to professional position?

LUDWIG
According to professional position!

JULIA
Then, horror!

ALL
Why, what's the matter? What's the matter? What's the matter?

SONG—**JULIA** (LISA clinging to her.)
Ah, pity me, my comrades true,
Who love, as well I know you do,
This gentle child,
To me so fondly dear!

ALL
Why, what's the matter?

JULIA
Our sister love so true and deep
From many an eye unused to weep
Hath oft beguiled
The coy reluctant tear!

ALL
Why, what's the matter?

JULIA
Each sympathetic heart 'twill bruise
When you have heard the frightful news
(O will it not?)
That I must now impart!

ALL
Why, what's the matter?

JULIA
Her love for him is all in all!
Ah, cursed fate! that it should fall
Unto my lot
To break my darling's heart!

ALL
Why, what's the matter?

LUDWIG
What means our Julia by those fateful looks?
Please do not keep us all on tenter-hooks-
Now, what's the matter?

JULIA.
Our duty, if we're wise,
We never shun.
This Spartan rule applies
To every one.
In theatres, as in life,
Each has her line—
This part—the Grand Duke's wife
(Oh agony!) is mine!
A maxim new I do not start—
The canons of dramatic art
Decree that this repulsive part
(The Grand Duke's wife)
Is mine!

ALL
Oh, that's the matter!

LISA (appalled, to LUDWIG).
Can that be so?

LUDWIG
I do not know—
But time will show
If that be so.

CHORUS
Can that be so? etc.

LISA (recit.)
Be merciful!

DUET—LISA and JULIA.

LISA
Oh, listen to me, dear—
I love him only, darling!
Remember, oh, my pet,
On him my heart is set
This kindness do me, dear-

Nor leave me lonely, darling!
Be merciful, my pet,
Our love do not forget!

JULIA
Now don't be foolish, dear—
You couldn't play it, darling!
It's "leading business", pet
And you're but a soubrette.
So don't be mulish, dear-
Although I say it, darling,
It's not your line, my pet—
I play that part, you bet!
I play that part—
I play that part, you bet!

(LISA overwhelmed with grief.)

NOTARY TANNHAUSER
The lady's right. Though Julia's engagement
Was for the stage meant—
It certainly frees Ludwig from his
Connubial promise.
Though marriage contracts—or whate'er you call 'em—
Are very solemn,
Dramatic contracts (which you all adore so)
Are even more so!

ALL
That's very true!
Though marriage contracts, etc.

SONG—**LISA**
The die is cast,
My hope has perished!
Farewell, O Past,
Too bright to last,
Yet fondly cherished!
My light has fled,
My hope is dead,
Its doom is spoken—
My day is night,
My wrong is right
In all men's sight—
My heart is broken!

[Exit weeping.

LUDWIG (recit.).
Poor child, where will she go? What will she do?

JULIA
That isn't in your part, you know.

LUDWIG (sighing).
Quite true!
(With an effort.) Depressing topics we'll not touch upon—
Let us begin as we are going on!
For this will be a jolly Court, for little and for big!

ALL
Sing hey, the jolly jinks of Pfennig Halbpfennig!

LUDWIG
From morn to night our lives shall be as merry as a grig!

ALL
Sing hey, the jolly jinks of Pfennig Halbpfennig!

LUDWIG
All state and ceremony we'll eternally abolish—
We don't mean to insist upon unnecessary polish—
And, on the whole, I rather think you'll find our rule tollolish!

ALL
Sing hey, the jolly jinks of Pfennig Halbpfennig!

JULIA
But stay—your new-made Court
Without a courtly coat is—
We shall require
Some Court attire,
And at a moment's notice.
In clothes of common sort
Your courtiers must not grovel—
Your new noblesse
Must have a dress
Original and novel!

LUDWIG
Old Athens we'll exhume!
The necessary dresses,
Correct and true
And all brand-new,
The company possesses:
Henceforth our Court costume

Shall live in song and story,
For we'll upraise
The dead old days
Of Athens in her glory!

ALL
Yes, let's upraise
The dead old days
Of Athens in her glory!

ALL
Agreed! Agreed!
For this will be a jolly Court for little and for big! etc

(They carry LUDWIG round stage and deposit him on the ironwork of well. JULIA stands by him, and the rest group round them.)

END OF ACT I.

ACT II

(THE NEXT MORNING.)

SCENE.—Entrance Hall of the Grand Ducal Palace.

Enter a procession of the members of the theatrical company (now dressed in the costumes of Troilus and Cressida), carrying garlands, playing on pipes, citharae, and cymbals, and heralding the return of LUDWIG and JULIA from the marriage ceremony, which has just taken place.

CHORUS
As before you we defile,
Eloia! Eloia!
Pray you, gentles, do not smile
If we shout, in classic style,
Eloia!
Ludwig and his Julia true
Wedded are each other to—
So we sing, till all is blue,
Eloia! Eloia!
Opoponax! Eloia!

Wreaths of bay and ivy twine,
Eloia! Eloia!
Fill the bowl with Lesbian wine,
And to revelry incline—

Eloia!

For as gaily we pass on
Probably we shall, anon,
Sing a Diergeticon—
Eloia! Eloia!
Opoponax! Eloia!

RECITATIVE—**LUDWIG**
Your loyalty our Ducal heartstrings touches:
Allow me to present your new Grand Duchess.
Should she offend, you'll graciously excuse her—
And kindly recollect I didn't choose her!

SONG—**LUDWIG**
At the outset I may mention it's my sovereign intention
To revive the classic memories of Athens at its best,
For the company possesses all the necessary dresses
And a course of quiet cramming will supply us with the rest.
We've a choir hyporchematic (that is, ballet-operatic)
Who respond to the choreut of that cultivated age,
And our clever chorus-master, all but captious criticaster
Would accept as the choregus of the early Attic stage.
This return to classic ages is considered in their wages,
Which are always calculated by the day or by the week—
And I'll pay 'em (if they'll back me) all in oboloi and drachm,
Which they'll get (if they prefer it) at the Kalends that are Greek!

(Confidentially to audience.)
At this juncture I may mention
That this erudition sham
Is but classical pretension,
The result of steady "cram.":
Periphrastic methods spurning,
To this audience discerning
I admit this show of learning
Is the fruit of steady "cram."!

CHORUS.
Periphrastic methods, etc.
In the period Socratic every dining-room was Attic
(Which suggests an architecture of a topsy-turvy kind),
There they'd satisfy their thirst on a recherche cold {Greek word}
Which is what they called their lunch—and so may you if you're inclined.
As they gradually got on, they'd {four Greek words)
(Which is Attic for a steady and a conscientious drink).
But they mixed their wine with water—which I'm sure they didn't oughter—
And we modern Saxons know a trick worth two of that, I think!

Then came rather risky dances (under certain circumstances)
Which would shock that worthy gentleman, the Licenser of Plays,
Corybantian maniac kick—Dionysiac or Bacchic—
And the Dithyrambic revels of those undecorous days.

(Confidentially to audience.)
And perhaps I'd better mention,
Lest alarming you I am,
That it isn't our intention
To perform a Dithyramb—
It displays a lot of stocking,
Which is always very shocking,
And of course I'm only mocking
At the prevalence of "cram"!

CHORUS
It displays a lot, etc.

Yes, on reconsideration, there are customs of that nation
Which are not in strict accordance with the habits of our day,
And when I come to codify, their rules I mean to modify,
Or Mrs. Grundy, p'r'aps, may have a word or two to say.
For they hadn't macintoshes or umbrellas or goloshes—
And a shower with their dresses must have played the very deuce,
And it must have been unpleasing when they caught a fit of sneezing,
For, it seems, of pocket-handkerchiefs they didn't know the use.
They wore little underclothing—scarcely anything—or nothing—
And their dress of Coan silk was quite transparent in design—
Well, in fact, in summer weather, something like the "altogether"
And it's there, I rather fancy, I shall have to draw the line!

(Confidentially to audience.)
And again I wish to mention
That this erudition sham
Is but classical pretension,
The result of steady "cram."
Yet my classic lore aggressive
(If you'll pardon the possessive)
Is exceedingly impressive
When you're passing an exam.

CHORUS
Yet his classic lore, etc.

[Exeunt CHORUS. Manent LUDWIG, JULIA, and LISA.

LUDWIG (recitative)
Yes, Ludwig and his Julia are mated!

For when an obscure comedian, whom the law backs,
To sovereign rank is promptly elevated,
He takes it with its incidental drawbacks!
So Julia and I are duly mated!

(LISA, through this, has expressed intense distress at having to surrender LUDWIG.)

SONG—**LISA**
Take care of him—he's much too good to live,
With him you must be very gentle:
Poor fellow, he's so highly sensitive,
And O, so sentimental!
Be sure you never let him sit up late
In chilly open air conversing—
Poor darling, he's extremely delicate,
And wants a deal of nursing!

LUDWIG
I want a deal of nursing!

LISA
And O, remember this—
When he is cross with pain,
A flower and a kiss—
A simple flower—a tender kiss
Will bring him round again!

His moods you must assiduously watch:
When he succumbs to sorrow tragic,
Some hardbake or a bit of butter-scotch
Will work on him like magic.
To contradict a character so rich
In trusting love were simple blindness—
He's one of those exalted natures which
Will only yield to kindness!

LUDWIG
I only yield to kindness!

LISA.
And O, the bygone bliss!
And O, the present pain!
That flower and that kiss—
That simple flower—that tender kiss
I ne'er shall give again!

[Exit, weeping.

JULIA
And now that everybody has gone, and we're happily and comfortably married, I want to have a few words with my new-born husband.

LUDWIG (aside).
Yes, I expect you'll often have a few words with your new-born husband! (Aloud.) Well, what is it?

JULIA
Why, I've been thinking that as you and I have to play our parts for life, it is most essential that we should come to a definite understanding as to how they shall be rendered. Now, I've been considering how I can make the most of the Grand Duchess.

LUDWIG
Have you? Well, if you'll take my advice, you'll make a very fine part of it.

JULIA
Why, that's quite my idea.

LUDWIG
I shouldn't make it one of your hoity-toity vixenish viragoes.

JULIA
You think not?

LUDWIG
Oh, I'm quite clear about that. I should make her a tender, gentle, submissive, affectionate (but not too affectionate) child-wife—timidly anxious to coil herself into her husband's heart, but kept in check by an awestruck reverence for his exalted intellectual qualities and his majestic personal appearance.

JULIA.
Oh, that is your idea of a good part?

LUDWIG
Yes—a wife who regards her husband's slightest wish as an inflexible law, and who ventures but rarely into his august presence, unless (which would happen seldom) he should summon her to appear before him. A crushed, despairing violet, whose blighted existence would culminate (all too soon) in a lonely and pathetic death-scene! A fine part, my dear.

JULIA
Yes. There's a good deal to be said for your view of it. Now there are some actresses whom it would fit like a glove.

LUDWIG (aside)
I wish I'd married one of 'em!

JULIA
But, you see, I must consider my temperament. For instance, my temperament would demand some strong scenes of justifiable jealousy.

LUDWIG

Oh, there's no difficulty about that. You shall have them.

JULIA

With a lovely but detested rival—

LUDWIG

Oh, I'll provide the rival.

JULIA

Whom I should stab—stab—stab!

LUDWIG

Oh, I wouldn't stab her. It's been done to death. I should treat her with a silent and contemptuous disdain, and delicately withdraw from a position which, to one of your sensitive nature, would be absolutely untenable. Dear me, I can see you delicately withdrawing, up centre and off!

JULIA

Can you?

LUDWIG

Yes. It's a fine situation—and in your hands, full of quiet pathos!

DUET—**LUDWIG and JULIA**

LUDWIG

Now Julia, come,
Consider it from
This dainty point of view—
A timid tender
Feminine gender,
Prompt to coyly coo—
Yet silence seeking,
Seldom speaking
Till she's spoken to—
A comfy, cosy,
Rosy-posy
Innocent ingenoo!
The part you're suited to—
(To give the deuce her due)
A sweet (O, jiminy!)
Miminy-piminy,
Innocent ingenoo!

ENSEMBLE.

LUDWIG   **JULIA.**

The part you're suited to—
(To give the deuce her due)
A sweet (O, jiminy!)
Miminy-piminy,
Innocent ingenoo!

I'm much obliged to you,
I don't think that would do—
To play (O, jiminy!)
Miminy-piminy,
Innocent ingenoo!

JULIA
You forget my special magic
(In a high dramatic sense)
Lies in situations tragic—
Undeniably intense.
As I've justified promotion
In the histrionic art,
I'll submit to you my notion
Of a first-rate part.

LUDWIG
Well, let us see your notion
Of a first-rate part.

JULIA (dramatically).
I have a rival! Frenzy-thrilled,
I find you both together!
My heart stands still—with horror chilled—-
Hard as the millstone nether!
Then softly, slyly, snaily, snaky—
Crawly, creepy, quaily, quaky—
I track her on her homeward way,
As panther tracks her fated prey!

(Furiously) I fly at her soft white throat—
The lily-white laughing leman!
On her agonized gaze I gloat
With the glee of a dancing demon!
My rival she—I have no doubt of her—-
So I hold on—till the breath is out of her!
—till the breath is out of her!

And then—Remorse! Remorse!
O cold unpleasant corse,
Avaunt! Avaunt!
That lifeless form
I gaze upon—
That face, still warm
But weirdly wan—
Those eyes of glass
I contemplate—
And then, alas!

Too late—too late!
I find she is—your Aunt!
(Shuddering.) Remorse! Remorse!

Then, mad—mad—mad!
With fancies wild—chimerical—
Now sorrowful—silent—sad—
Now hullaballoo hysterical!
Ha! ha! ha! ha!
But whether I'm sad or whether I'm glad,
Mad! mad! mad! mad!

This calls for the resources of a high-class art,
And satisfies my notion of a first-rate part!

[Exit JULIA

Enter all the CHORUS, hurriedly, and in great excitement.

CHORUS
Your Highness, there's a party at the door—
Your Highness, at the door there is a party—
She says that we expect her,
But we do not recollect her,
For we never saw her countenance before!

With rage and indignation she is rife,
Because our welcome wasn't very hearty—
She's as sulky as a super,
And she's swearing like a trooper,
O, you never heard such language in your life!

Enter BARONESS VON KRAKENFELDT, in a fury.

BARONESS VON KRAKENFELDT
With fury indescribable I burn!
With rage I'm nearly ready to explode!
There'll be grief and tribulation when I learn
To whom this slight unbearable is owed!
For whatever may be due I'll pay it double—
There'll be terror indescribable and trouble!
With a hurly-burly and a hubble-bubble
I'll pay you for this pretty episode!

ALL
Oh, whatever may be due she'll pay it double!—
It's very good of her to take the trouble—
But we don't know what she means by "hubble-bubble"—

No doubt it's an expression la mode.

BARONESS VON KRAKENFELDT (to LUDWIG).
Do you know who I am?

LUDWIG (examining her).
I don't;
Your countenance I can't fix, my dear.

BARONESS VON KRAKENFELDT
This proves I'm not a sham.

(Showing pocket-handkerchief.)

LUDWIG (examining it).
It won't;
It only says "Krakenfeldt, Six," my dear.

BARONESS VON KRAKENFELDT
Express your grief profound!

LUDWIG
I shan't!
This tone I never allow, my love.

BARONESS VON KRAKENFELDT
Rudolph at once produce!

LUDWIG
I can't;
He isn't at home just now, my love.

BARONESS VON KRAKENFELDT (astonished).
He isn't at home just now!

ALL
He isn't at home just now,
(Dancing derisively.)
He has an appointment particular, very—
You'll find him, I think, in the town cemetery;
And that's how we come to be making so merry,
For he isn't at home just now!

BARONESS VON KRAKENFELDT
But bless my heart and soul alive, it's impudence personified!
I've come here to be matrimonially matrimonified!

LUDWIG

For any disappointment I am sorry unaffectedly,
But yesterday that nobleman expired quite unexpectedly—

ALL (sobbing).
Tol the riddle lol!
Tol the riddle lol!
Tol the riddle, lol the riddle, lol lol lay!
(Then laughing wildly.)
Tol the riddle, lol the riddle, lol lol lay!

BARONESS VON KRAKENFELDT
But this is most unexpected. He was well enough at a quarter to twelve yesterday.

LUDWIG
Yes. He died at half-past eleven.

BARONESS VON KRAKENFELDT
Bless me, how very sudden!

LUDWIG
It was sudden.

BARONESS VON KRAKENFELDT
But what in the world am I to do? I was to have been married to him to-day!

ALL (singing and dancing).
For any disappointment we are sorry unaffectedly,
But yesterday that nobleman expired quite unexpectedly—
Tol the riddle lol!

BARONESS VON KRAKENFELDT
Is this Court Mourning or a Fancy Ball?

LUDWIG
Well, it's a delicate combination of both effects. It is intended to express inconsolable grief for the decease of the late Duke and ebullient joy at the accession of his successor. I am his successor. Permit me to present you to my Grand Duchess.

(Indicating JULIA.)

BARONESS VON KRAKENFELDT
Your Grand Duchess? Oh, your Highness!

(Curtseying profoundly.)

JULIA (sneering at her)
Old frump!

BARONESS VON KRAKENFELDT

Humph! A recent creation, probably?

LUDWIG

We were married only half an hour ago.

BARONESS VON KRAKENFELDT

Exactly. I thought she seemed new to the position.

JULIA.

Ma'am, I don't know who you are, but I flatter myself I can do justice to any part on the very shortest notice.

BARONESS VON KRAKENFELDT

My dear, under the circumstances you are doing admirably—and you'll improve with practice. It's so difficultto be a lady when one isn't born to it.

JULIA (in a rage, to LUDWIG)

Am I to stand this? Am I not to be allowed to pull her to pieces?

LUDWIG (aside to JULIA)

No, no—it isn't Greek. Be a violet, I beg.

BARONESS VON KRAKENFELDT

And now tell me all about this distressing circumstance. How did the Grand Duke die?

LUDWIG

He perished nobly—in a Statutory Duel.

BARONESS VON KRAKENFELDT

In a Statutory Duel? But that's only a civil death!—and the Act expires to-night, and then he will come to life again!

LUDWIG

Well, no. Anxious to inaugurate my reign by conferring some inestimable boon on my people, I signalized this occasion by reviving the law for another hundred years.

BARONESS VON KRAKENFELDT

For another hundred years? Then set the merry joybells ringing! Let festive epithalamia resound through these ancient halls! Cut the satisfying sandwich—broach the exhilarating Marsala—and let us rejoice to-day, if we never rejoice again!

LUDWIG

But I don't think I quite understand. We have already rejoiced a good deal.

BARONESS VON KRAKENFELDT

Happy man, you little reck of the extent of the good things you are in for. When you killed Rudolph you adopted all his overwhelming responsibilities. Know then that I, Caroline von Krakenfeldt, am the most overwhelming of them all!

LUDWIG
But stop, stop—I've just been married to somebody else!

JULIA
Yes, ma'am, to somebody else, ma'am! Do you understand, ma'am? To somebody else!

BARONESS VON KRAKENFELDT
Do keep this young woman quiet; she fidgets me!

JULIA
Fidgets you!

LUDWIG (aside to JULIA)
Be a violet—a crushed, despairing violet.

JULIA
Do you suppose I intend to give up a magnificent part without a struggle?

LUDWIG
My good girl, she has the law on her side. Let us both bear this calamity with resignation. If you must struggle, go away and struggle in the seclusion of your chamber.

SONG—**BARONESS and CHORUS**
Now away to the wedding we go,
So summon the charioteers—
No kind of reluctance they show
To embark on their married careers.
Though Julia's emotion may flow
For the rest of her maidenly years,

ALL
To the wedding we eagerly go,
So summon the charioteers!

Now away, etc.

(All dance off to wedding except JULIA.)

RECITATIVE—**JULIA**

So ends my dream—so fades my vision fair!
Of hope no gleam—distraction and despair!
My cherished dream, the Ducal throne to share
That aim supreme has vanished into air!

SONG—**JULIA**
Broken every promise plighted—
All is darksome—all is dreary.
Every new-born hope is blighted!
Sad and sorry—weak and weary
Death the Friend or Death the Foe,
Shall I call upon thee? No!
I will go on living, though
Sad and sorry—weak and weary!

No, no! Let the bygone go by!
No good ever came of repining:
If to-day there are clouds o'er the sky,
To-morrow the sun may be shining!
To-morrow, be kind,
To-morrow, to me!
With loyalty blind
I curtsey to thee!
To-day is a day of illusion and sorrow,
So viva To-morrow, To-morrow, To-morrow!
God save you, To-morrow!
Your servant, To-morrow!
God save you, To-morrow, To-morrow, To-morrow!

[Exit JULIA.

Enter ERNEST.

ERNEST
It's of no use—I can't wait any longer. At any risk I must gratify my urgent desire to know what is going on. (Looking off.) Why, what's that? Surely I see a wedding procession winding down the hill, dressed in my Troilus and Cressida costumes! That's Ludwig's doing! I see how it is—he found the time hang heavy on his hands, and is amusing himself by getting married to Lisa. No—it can't be to Lisa, for here she is!

Enter LISA.

LISA (not seeing him).
I really cannot stand seeing my
Ludwig married twice in one day to somebody else!

ERNEST
Lisa!

(LISA sees him, and stands as if transfixed with horror.).

ERNEST
Come here—don't be a little fool—I want you.

(LISA suddenly turns and bolts off.)

ERNEST
Why, what's the matter with the little donkey? One would think she saw a ghost! But if he's not marrying Lisa, whom is he marrying? (Suddenly.) Julia! (Much overcome.) I see it all! The scoundrel! He had to adopt all my responsibilities, and he's shabbily taken advantage of the situation to marry the girl I'm engaged to! But no, it can't be Julia, for here she is!

Enter JULIA.

JULIA (not seeing him).
I've made up my mind. I won't stand it! I'll send in my notice at once!

ERNEST
Julia! Oh, what a relief!

(JULIA gazes at him as if transfixed.)

ERNEST
Then you've not married Ludwig? You are still true to me?

(JULIA turns and bolts in grotesque horror. ERNEST follows and stops her.)

ERNEST
Don't run away! Listen to me. Are you all crazy?

JULIA (in affected terror)
What would you with me, spectre? Oh, ain't his eyes sepulchral! And ain't his voice hollow! What are you doing out of your tomb at this time of day—apparition?

ERNEST
I do wish I could make you girls understand that I'm only technically dead, and that physically I'm as much alive as ever I was in my life!

JULIA
Oh, but it's an awful thing to be haunted by a technical bogy!

ERNEST
You won't be haunted much longer. The law must be on its last legs, and in a few hours I shall come to life again—resume all my social and civil functions, and claim my darling as my blushing bride!

JULIA
Oh—then you haven't heard?

ERNEST
My love, I've heard nothing. How could I? There are no daily papers where I come from.

JULIA

Why, Ludwig challenged Rudolph and won, and now he's Grand Duke, and he's revived the law for another century!

ERNEST

What! But you're not serious—you're only joking!

JULIA

My good sir, I'm a light-hearted girl, but I don't chaff bogies.

ERNEST

Well, that's the meanest dodge I ever heard of!

JULIA

Shabby trick, I call it.

ERNEST

But you don't mean to say that you're going to cry off!

JULIA

I really can't afford to wait until your time is up.
You know, I've always set my face against long engagements.

ERNEST

Then defy the law and marry me now. We will fly to your native country, and I'll play broken-English in London as you play broken-German here!

JULIA.

No. These legal technicalities cannot be defied. Situated as you are, you have no power to make me your wife. At best you could only make me your widow.

ERNEST

Then be my widow—my little, dainty, winning, winsome widow!

JULIA

Now what would be the good of that? Why, you goose, I should marry again within a month!

DUET—**ERNEST and JULIA**

ERNEST

If the light of love's lingering ember
Has faded in gloom,
You cannot neglect, O remember,
A voice from the tomb!
That stern supernatural diction
Should act as a solemn restriction,
Although by a mere legal fiction
A voice from the tomb!

JULIA (in affected terror).
I own that that utterance chills me—
It withers my bloom!
With awful emotion it thrills me—
That voice from the tomb!
Oh, spectre, won't anything lay thee?
Though pained to deny or gainsay thee,
In this case I cannot obey thee,
Thou voice from the tomb!

(Dancing.)
So, spectre, appalling,
I bid you good-day—
Perhaps you'll be calling
When passing this way.
Your bogydom scorning,
And all your love-lorning,
I bid you good-morning,
I bid you good-day.

ERNEST (furious).
My offer recalling,
Your words I obey—
Your fate is appalling,
And full of dismay.
To pay for this scorning
I give you fair warning
I'll haunt you each morning,
Each night, and each day!

(Repeat ENSEMBLE, and exeunt in opposite directions.)

Re-enter the WEDDING PROCESSION dancing.

CHORUS
Now bridegroom and bride let us toast
In a magnum of merry champagne—
Let us make of this moment the most,
We may not be so lucky again.
So drink to our sovereign host
And his highly intelligent reign—
His health and his bride's let us toast
In a magnum of merry champagne!

SONG—**BARONESS with CHORUS**
I once gave an evening party
(A sandwich and cut-orange ball),

But my guests had such appetites hearty
That I couldn't enjoy it, enjoy it at all.
I made a heroic endeavour
To look unconcerned, but in vain,
And I vow'd that I never—oh never
Would ask anybody again!
But there's a distinction decided—-
A difference truly immense—
When the wine that you drink is provided, provided,
At somebody else's expense.
So bumpers—aye, ever so many—
The cost we may safely ignore!
For the wine doesn't cost us a penny,
Tho' it's Pommry seventy-four!

CHORUS
So bumpers—aye, ever so many—etc.
Come, bumpers—aye, ever so many—
And then, if you will, many more!
This wine doesn't cost us a penny,
Tho' it's Pommry, Pommry seventy-four!
Old wine is a true panacea
For ev'ry conceivable ill,
When you cherish the soothing idea
That somebody else pays the bill!
Old wine is a pleasure that's hollow
When at your own table you sit,
For you're thinking each mouthful you swallow
Has cost you, has cost you a threepenny-bit!
So bumpers—aye, ever so many—
And then, if you will, many more!
This wine doesn't cost us a penny,
Tho' it's Pommry seventy-four!

CHORUS
So, bumpers—aye, ever so many—etc.

(March heard.)

LUDWIG (recitative).
Why, who is this approaching,
Upon our joy encroaching?
Some rascal come a-poaching
Who's heard that wine we're broaching?

ALL
Who may this be?
Who may this be?

Who is he? Who is he? Who is he?

Enter HERALD.

HERALD
The Prince of Monte Carlo,
From Mediterranean water,
Has come here to bestow
On you his beautiful daughter.
They've paid off all they owe,
As every statesman oughter—
That Prince of Monte Carlo
And his be-eautiful daughter!

CHORUS
The Prince of Monte Carlo, etc.

HERALD
The Prince of Monte Carlo,
Who is so very partickler,
Has heard that you're also
For ceremony a stickler—
Therefore he lets you know
By word of mouth auric'lar—
(That Prince of Monte Carlo
Who is so very particklar)—

CHORUS
The Prince of Monte Carlo, etc.

HERALD
That Prince of Monte Carlo,
From Mediterranean water,
Has come here to bestow
On you his be-eautiful daughter!

LUDWIG (recitative).
His Highness we know not—nor the locality
In which is situate his Principality;
But, as he guesses by some odd fatality,
This is the shop for cut and dried formality!
Let him appear—
He'll find that we're
Remarkable for cut and dried formality.

(Reprise of March. Exit HERALD.

LUDWIG beckons his Court.)

LUDWIG
I have a plan—I'll tell you all the plot of it—
He wants formality—he shall have a lot of it!
(Whispers to them, through symphony.)
Conceal yourselves, and when I give the cue,
Spring out on him—you all know what to do!

(All conceal themselves behind the draperies that enclose the stage.)

Pompous March.

Enter the PRINCE and PRINCESS OF MONTE CARLO, attended by six theatrical-looking nobles and the Court Costumier.

DUET—**PRINCE and PRINCESS**

PRINCE
We're rigged out in magnificent array
(Our own clothes are much gloomier)
In costumes which we've hired by the day
From a very well-known costumier.

COSTUMIER (bowing).
I am the well-known costumier.

PRINCESS
With a brilliant staff a Prince should make a show
(It's a rule that never varies),
So we've engaged from the Theatre Monaco
Six supernumeraries.

NOBLES
We're the supernumeraries.

ALL
At a salary immense,
Quite regardless of expense,
Six supernumeraries!

PRINCE
They do not speak, for they break our grammar's laws,
And their language is lamentable—
And they never take off their gloves, because
Their nails are not presentable.

NOBLES
Our nails are not presentable!

PRINCESS
To account for their shortcomings manifest
We explain, in a whisper bated,
They are wealthy members of the brewing interest
To the Peerage elevated.

NOBLES
To the Peerage elevated.

ALL
They're/We're very, very rich,
And accordingly, as sich,
To the Peerage elevated.

PRINCE
Well, my dear, here we are at last—just in time to compel Duke Rudolph to fulfil the terms of his marriage contract. Another hour and we should have been too late.

PRINCESS
Yes, papa, and if you hadn't fortunately discovered a means of making an income by honest industry, we should never have got here at all.

PRINCE
Very true. Confined for the last two years within the precincts of my palace by an obdurate bootmaker who held a warrant for my arrest, I devoted my enforced leisure to a study of the doctrine of chances—mainly with the view of ascertaining whether there was the remotest chance of my ever going out for a walk again—and this led to the discovery of a singularly fascinating little round game which I have called Roulette, and by which, in one sitting, I won no less than five thousand francs! My first act was to pay my bootmaker—my second, to engage a good useful working set of second-hand nobles—and my third, to hurry you off to Pfennig Halbpfennig as fast as a train de luxe could carry us!

PRINCESS
Yes, and a pretty job-lot of second-hand nobles you've scraped together!

PRINCE (doubtfully)
Pretty, you think? Humph! I don't know. I should say tol-lol, my love—only tol-lol. They are not wholly satisfactory. There is a certain air of unreality about them—they are not convincing.

COSTUMIER
But, my goot friend, vhat can you expect for eighteenpence a day!

PRINCE
Now take this Peer, for instance. What the deuce do you call him?

COSTUMIER
Him? Oh, he's a swell—he's the Duke of Riviera.

PRINCE

Oh, he's a Duke, is he? Well, that's no reason Why he should look so confoundedly haughty. (To NOBLE) Be affable, sir! (NOBLE takes attitude of affability.) That's better. (Passing to another.) Now, who's this with his moustache coming off?

COSTUMIER

Vhy; you're Viscount Mentone, ain't you?

NOBLE

Blest if I know. (Turning up sword-belt.) It's wrote here—yes, Viscount Mentone.

COSTUMIER

Then vhy don't you say so? 'Old yerself up—you ain't carryin' sandwich boards now.

(Adjusts his moustache.)

PRINCE

Now, once for all, you Peers—when His Highness arrives, don't stand like sticks, but appear to take an intelligent and sympathetic interest in what is going on. You needn't say anything, but let your gestures be in accordance with the spirit of the conversation. Now take the word from me. Affability! (attitude). Submission! (attitude). Surprise! (attitude). Shame! (attitude). Grief! (attitude). Joy! (attitude). That's better! You can do it if you like!

PRINCESS

But, papa, where in the world is the Court? There is positively no one here to receive us! I can't help feeling that Rudolph wants to get out of it because I'm poor. He's a miserly little wretch—that's what he is.

PRINCE

Well, I shouldn't go so far as to say that. I should rather describe him as an enthusiastic collector of coins—of the realm—and we must not be too hard upon a numismatist if he feels a certain disinclination to part with some of his really very valuable specimens. It's a pretty hobby: I've often thought I should like to collect some coins myself.

PRINCESS

Papa, I'm sure there's some one behind that curtain. I saw it move!

PRINCE

Then no doubt they are coming. Now mind, you Peers—haughty affability combined with a sense of what is due to your exalted ranks, or I'll fine you half a franc each—upon my soul I will!

(Gong. The curtains fly back and the COURT are discovered. They give a wild yell and rush on to the stage dancing wildly, with PRINCE, PRINCESS, and Nobles, who are taken by surprise at first, but eventually join in a reckless dance. At the end all fall down exhausted.)

LUDWIG

There, what do you think of that? That's our official ceremonial for the reception of visitors of the very highest distinction.

PRINCE (puzzled)
It's very quaint—very curious indeed.
Prettily footed, too. Prettily footed.

LUDWIG
Would you like to see how we say "good-bye" to visitors of distinction? That ceremony is also performed with the foot.

PRINCE
Really, this tone—ah, but perhaps you have not completely grasped the situation?

LUDWIG
Not altogether.

PRINCE
Ah, then I'll give you a lead over.
(Significantly:) I am the father of the Princess of Monte Carlo.
Doesn't that convey any idea to the Grand Ducal mind?

LUDWIG (stolidly)
Nothing definite.

PRINCE (aside)
H'm—very odd! Never mind—try again!
(Aloud.) This is the daughter of the Prince of Monte Carlo. Do you take?

LUDWIG (still puzzled)
No—not yet. Go on—don't give it up—I dare say it will come presently.

PRINCE
Very odd—never mind—try again. (With sly significance.) Twenty years ago! Little doddle doddle! Two little doddle doddles! Happy father—hers and yours. Proud mother—yours and hers! Hah! Now you take? I see you do! I see you do!

LUDWIG
Nothing is more annoying than to feel that you're not equal to the intellectual pressure of the conversation. I wish he'd say something intelligible.

PRINCE
You didn't expect me?

LUDWIG (jumping at it)
No, no. I grasp that—thank you very much. (Shaking hands with him.) No, I did not expect you!

PRINCE

I thought not. But ha! ha! at last I have escaped from my enforced restraint. (General movement of alarm.) (To crowd who are stealing off.) No, no—you misunderstand me. I mean I've paid my debts!

ALL
Oh! (They return.)

PRINCESS (affectionately)
But, my darling, I'm afraid that even now you don't quite realize who I am!

(Embracing him.)

BARONESS
Why, you forward little hussy, how dare you?

(Takes her away from LUDWIG.)

LUDWIG
You mustn't do that, my dear—never in the presence of the Grand Duchess, I beg!

PRINCESS (weeping)
Oh, papa, he's got a Grand Duchess!

LUDWIG
A Grand Duchess! My good girl, I've got three Grand Duchesses!

PRINCESS
Well, I'm sure! Papa, let's go away—this is not a respectable Court.

PRINCE
All these Grand Dukes have their little fancies, My love. This potentate appears to be collecting wives. It's a pretty hobby—I should like to collect a few myself. This (admiring BARONESS) is a charming specimen—an antique, I should say—of the early Merovingian period, if I'm not mistaken; and here's another—a Scotch lady, I think (alluding to JULIA), and (alluding to LISA) a little one thrown in. Two half-quarterns and a makeweight! (To LUDWIG.) Have you such a thing as a catalogue of the Museum?

PRINCESS
But I cannot permit Rudolph to keep a museum—

LUDWIG
Rudolph? Get along with you, I'm not Rudolph!
Rudolph died yesterday!

PRINCE and PRINCESS
What!

LUDWIG
Quite suddenly—of—of—a cardiac affection.

PRINCE and PRINCESS
Of a cardiac affection!

LUDWIG
Yes, a pack-of-cardiac affection. He fought a Statutory Duel with me and lost, and I took over all his engagements—including this imperfectly preserved old lady, to whom he has been engaged for the last three weeks.

PRINCESS
Three weeks! But I've been engaged to him for the last twenty years!

BARONESS, LISA, and JULIA
Twenty years!

PRINCE (aside)
It's all right, my love—they can't get over that. (Aloud.) He's yours—take him, and hold him as tight as you can!

PRINCESS
My own!

(Embracing LUDWIG.)

LUDWIG
Here's another!—the fourth in four-and-twenty hours!
Would anybody else like to marry me? You, ma'am—or you—anybody! I'm getting used to it!

BARONESS
But let me tell you, ma'am—

JULIA
Why, you impudent little hussy—

LISA
Oh, here's another—here's another! (Weeping.)

PRINCESS
Poor ladies, I'm very sorry for you all; but, you see, I've a prior claim. Come, away we go—there's not a moment to be lost!

CHORUS (as they dance towards exit).
Away to the wedding we'll go
To summon the charioteers,
No kind of reluctance we show
To embark on our married careers—

(At this moment RUDOLPH, ERNEST, and NOTARY appear. All kneel in astonishment.)

RECITATIVE.

RUDOLPH
Ernest and Notary.
Forbear! This may not be!
Frustrated are your plans!
With paramount decree
The Law forbids the banns!

ALL
The Law forbids the banns!

LUDWIG
Not a bit of it! I've revived the law for another century!

RUDOLPH
You didn't revive it! You couldn't revive it!
You—you are an impostor, sir—a tuppenny rogue, sir! You—you never were, and in all human probability never will be—Grand Duke of Pfennig Anything!

ALL
What!!!

RUDOLPH
Never—never, never! (Aside.) Oh, my internal economy!

LUDWIG
That's absurd, you know. I fought the Grand Duke.
He drew a King, and I drew an Ace. He perished in inconceivable agonies on the spot. Now, as that's settled, we'll go on with the wedding.

RUDOLPH
It—it isn't settled. You—you can't. I—I—(to NOTARY). Oh, tell him—tell him! I can't!

NOTARY TANNHAUSER
Well, the fact is, there's been a little mistake here. On reference to the Act that regulates Statutory Duels, I find it is expressly laid down that the Ace shall count invariably as lowest!

ALL
As lowest!

RUDOLPH (breathlessly)
As lowest—lowest—lowest! So you're the ghoest—ghoest—ghoest! (Aside.) Oh, what is the matter with me inside here!

ERNEST
Well, Julia, as it seems that the law hasn't been revived—and as, consequently, I shall come to life in about three minutes—(consulting his watch)—

JULIA.

My objection falls to the ground. (Resignedly.)
Very well!

PRINCESS

And am I to understand that I was on the point of marrying a dead man without knowing it? (To
RUDOLPH, who revives.) Oh, my love, what a narrow escape I've had!

RUDOLPH

Oh—you are the Princess of Monte Carlo, and you've turned up just in time! Well, you're an attractive
little girl, you know, but you're as poor as a rat!

(They retire up together.)

LISA

That's all very well, but what is to become of me?
(To LUDWIG.) If you're a dead man—(Clock strikes three.)

LUDWIG

But I'm not. Time's up—the Act has expired—I've come to life—the parson is still in attendance, and
we'll all be married directly.

ALL

Hurrah!

FINALE

Happy couples, lightly treading,
Castle chapel will be quite full!
Each shall have a pretty wedding,
As, of course, is only rightful,
Though the brides be fair or frightful.
Contradiction little dreading,
This will be a day delightful—
Each shall have a pretty wedding!
Such a pretty, pretty wedding!
Such a pretty wedding!

(All dance off to get married as the curtain falls.)

CURTAIN

W.S. Gilbert – A Short Biography

Sir William Schwenck Gilbert was born on November 18th, 1836 at 17 Southampton Street, Strand,
London. His father, also named William, was a naval surgeon, who later became a writer of novels and

short stories, some of which were illustrated by his son. Gilbert's mother was the former Anne Mary Bye Morris (1812–1888), the daughter of Thomas Morris, an apothecary.

Gilbert's parents were distant and stern, and there was no close bond between either themselves or their children (the marriage was to eventually break up in 1876). Gilbert had three younger sisters, Jane Morris, Anne Maude Mary Florence.

As a child, Gilbert was nicknamed "Bab".

The family travelled to Italy in 1838 and then France before finally returning to settle in London in 1847.

Gilbert was educated in Boulogne, France from age seven, then at Western Grammar School, Brompton, London, before the Great Ealing School, where he became head boy and wrote plays for school performances. He then attended King's College London, graduating in 1856.

His first thought for a career was to take examinations for a commission in the Royal Artillery, but the Crimean War had just ended and with fewer recruits needed only a commission in a line regiment was available. He opted instead for the Civil Service and was an assistant clerk in the Privy Council Office for four years. He hated it. In 1859 he joined the Militia, a part-time volunteer force, and served until 1878, as his other work allowed, and reached the rank of Captain.

To supplement his income Gilbert wrote a variety of stories, comic rants, theatre reviews (many in the form of a parody of the play being reviewed), and, using the pseudonym of his childhood nickname, "Bab" illustrated poems for several comic magazines, primarily Fun, started in 1861. His work was also published in the Cornhill Magazine, London Society, Tinsley's Magazine and Temple Bar. Gilbert was also the London correspondent for L'Invalide Russe and a drama critic for the Illustrated London Times. In the 1860s he also contributed to Tom Hood's Christmas annuals, to Saturday Night, the Comic News and the Savage Club Papers.

The poems, illustrated humorously by Gilbert, proved immensely popular and were reprinted in book form as the Bab Ballads. He would later return to many of these as source material for his plays and comic operas.

In 1863 he received a bequest of £300 allowing him to leave the civil service and attempt a career as a barrister. Unfortunately, he managed to attract few clients.

However, these events happily coincided with his first professionally produced play; Uncle Baby, which ran for seven weeks in the autumn of 1863.

In 1865–66, Gilbert collaborated with Charles Millward on several pantomimes, including Hush-a-Bye, Baby, On the Tree Top, or, Harlequin Fortunia, King Frog of Frog Island, and the Magic Toys of Lowther Arcade (1866).

Gilbert's first solo success, however, came a few days after Hush-a-Bye Baby premiered. His friend and mentor, Tom Robertson, was asked to deliver a pantomime within two weeks. Robertson couldn't and recommended Gilbert who took the job. Written and rushed to the stage in 10 days, Dulcamara, or the Little Duck and the Great Quack, a burlesque of Gaetano Donizetti's L'elisir d'amore, proved very popular. This led to a long series of further Gilbert opera burlesques, pantomimes and farces, full of dreadful puns, but showing signs of the satire that would later be such an integral part of Gilbert's work.

After a failed relationship with the novelist Annie Thomas, Gilbert married Lucy Agnes Turner, whom he affectionately called "Kitty", in 1867; she was 11 years his junior. They were socially active both in London and later at their new home at Grim's Dyke, often holding dinner parties. Although they had no children they had many pets, including several exotic ones.

Next followed Gilbert's biggest success so far; his penultimate operatic parody, Robert the Devil, a burlesque of Giacomo Meyerbeer's opera, Robert le diable, part of a triple bill that opened the Gaiety Theatre, London in 1868. It ran for over 100 nights.

In Victorian theatre, Gilbert's burlesques were considered very tasteful compared to the offerings of others. He would now move away from burlesque to plays with original plots and fewer puns. His first was An Old Score in 1869.

Theatre, at this time had fallen into disrepute. London was awash with poorly translated French operettas and cheaply written, prurient Victorian burlesques. From 1869 to 1875, Gilbert joined with Thomas German Reed (and his wife Priscilla), whose Gallery of Illustration sought to regain some of theatre's lost respect with family entertainments. This would be so successful that by 1885 Gilbert could safely state that original British plays were appropriate for an innocent 15-year-old girl to watch.

The initial work for the Gallery of Illustration, No Cards, was the first of six musical entertainments for the German Reeds, by Gilbert some with music composed by Thomas German Reed.

The German Reeds' intimate theatre allowed Gilbert to develop a personal style that would also cede to him control all aspects of production; set, costumes, direction and stage management.

Gilbert's first big hit at the Gallery of Illustration, Ages Ago, also opened in 1869. It marked the beginning of a collaboration with the composer Frederic Clay that would last seven years and cover four works. It was at a rehearsal for Ages Ago that Clay introduced Gilbert to Arthur Sullivan.

These musical works gave Gilbert a valuable education as a lyricist and he perfected the 'topsy-turvy' style that he had been developing in his Bab Ballads, where the humour was derived by setting up a ridiculous premise and following through on its logical consequences, however absurd they might be.

Ever busy he found time to create several 'fairy comedies' at the Haymarket Theatre. The premise was the idea of self-revelation by characters under the influence of magic or some supernatural experience. The first was The Palace of Truth (1870), based partly on a story by Madame de Genlis. In 1871, with Pygmalion and Galatea, one of seven plays that he produced that year, Gilbert scored his greatest hit to date. Together, these plays including The Wicked World (1873), Sweethearts (1874), and Broken Hearts (1875), did for Gilbert on the dramatic stage what the German Reed entertainments had done for him on the musical stage: they established that his talents were large and burgeoning, a writer of wide range, as comfortable with human drama as much as farcical humour.

Contemptorous with this period Gilbert pushed the satirical boundaries. He collaborated with Gilbert Arthur à Beckett on The Happy Land (1873), in part, a parody of his own The Wicked World, which was briefly banned because of its caricatures of Gladstone and his ministers. Similarly, The Realm of Joy

(1873) was set in the lobby of a theatre performing a scandalous play (implied to be the Happy Land), with many jokes at the expense of the Lord Chamberlain (the "Lord High Disinfectant", as he's referred to in the play). In Charity (1874), however, Gilbert uses the freedom of the stage in a different way: to illuminate the contrasting ways in which society treated men and women who had sex outside of marriage. It was ground breaking and some see it as anticipating the 'problem plays' of Shaw and Ibsen.

Once established as a writer Gilbert was also the stage director, with strong, forceful opinions on how they should best be performed.

In Gilbert's 1874 burlesque, Rosencrantz and Guildenstern, the character Hamlet, in his speech to the players, sums up Gilbert's theory of comic acting: "I hold that there is no such antick fellow as your bombastical hero who doth so earnestly spout forth his folly as to make his hearers believe that he is unconscious of all incongruity". Again some say with this he prepared the ground for playwrights such as George Bernard Shaw and Oscar Wilde to be able to flourish.

Tom Robertson had "introduced Gilbert both to the revolutionary notion of disciplined rehearsals and to mise-en-scène or unity of style in the whole presentation – direction, design, music, acting." Like Robertson, Gilbert demanded discipline in his actors, that they know their lines, enunciate them clearly and keep to his stage directions, a new development for actors at the time. It also ushered in the replacement of the star with the disciplined ensemble.

Gilbert was meticulous in his preparations, making models of the stage and designing every action in advance. He refused to work with actors who challenged him. He was famous for demonstrating the action himself, even as he grew older. Such was his interest in standards that even during long runs and revivals, he closely supervised the performances of his plays, making sure that no one made additions or deletions.

Arthur Sullivan – A Short Biography

Sir Arthur Seymour Sullivan, MVO was born on May 13th 1842 in Lambeth, London. His father, Thomas Sullivan, a military bandmaster, clarinetist and music teacher, was born in Ireland and raised in Chelsea, London, and his mother, Mary Clementina (née Coghlan, English born, of Irish and Italian descent. Thomas Sullivan was based from 1845 to 1857 at the Royal Military College, Sandhurst, where he was the bandmaster and taught music privately to supplement his income. Young Sullivan became proficient with many of the instruments in the band and had composed an anthem, "By the waters of Babylon", by the age of eight. While proudly observing his son's obvious musical talent, he knew, at first hand, how insecure a profession it was and discouraged him from pursuing it.

Three years later whilst at a private school in Bayswater, Sullivan persuaded his parents and headmaster to allow him to apply for membership in the choir of the Chapel Royal. There were concerns that Sullivan at nearly 12 years of age was too old to be a treble as his voice would soon break. But he was accepted and soon became a soloist and, by 1856, was promoted to "first boy". Troublingly, even at this age, Sullivan's health was delicate, and he was easily fatigued.

However, Sullivan flourished under the training of the Reverend Thomas Helmore, and began to compose anthems and songs. Helmore arranged for one pieces, "O Israel", to be published in 1855.

In 1856, the Royal Academy of Music awarded the first Mendelssohn Scholarship to the 14-year-old Sullivan, granting him a year's training at the academy. His principal teacher there was John Goss, whose own teacher had been a pupil of Mozart. Initially Sullivan studied piano.

Sullivan's scholarship was extended to a second year, and then a third so that he could study in Germany, at the Leipzig Conservatoire. There he was trained in Mendelssohn's ideas and techniques as well as being exposed to Schubert, Verdi, Bach, and Wagner. Sullivan was an eager pupil and always looking for inspiration. On a visit to a synagogue, he was so struck by some of the cadences and progressions in the music that three decades later he would recall them for use in his serious opera, Ivanhoe.

Though the scholarship in Leipzig, was for one year he stayed for three. Sullivan credited his Leipzig period with rapid and sustained musical growth. His graduation piece, in 1861, was a set of incidental music to Shakespeare's The Tempest. Revised and expanded, it was performed at the Crystal Palace in 1862, a year after his return to London. It was an immediate sensation. He began building a reputation as England's most promising young composer.

He now embarked on composing with a series of ambitious works, interspersed with hymns, parlour songs and other light pieces of a more commercial nature. These compositions could not support him financially, and from 1861 to 1872 he supplemented his income working as a church organist, a task he enjoyed, and as a music teacher, sometimes at the Crystal Palace School, which he hated and gave up as soon as his finances allowed. Sullivan also took an early chance to compose pieces for royalty with the wedding of the Prince of Wales in 1863.

Sullivan began to put voice and orchestra together with The Masque at Kenilworth (Birmingham Festival, 1864). For Covent Garden that same year he composed his first ballet, L'Île Enchantée.

1865 saw Sullivan initiated into Freemasonry and was Grand Organist of the United Grand Lodge of England in 1887 during Queen Victoria's Golden Jubilee.

In 1866, he premiered his Irish Symphony and Cello Concerto, his only works in these genres. In the same year, his Overture in C (In Memoriam), commemorating the recent death of his father, was a commission from the Norwich Festival.

His overture Marmion was premiered by the Philharmonic Society in 1867. The Times called it "another step in advance on the part of the only composer of any remarkable promise that just at present we can boast."

Sadly, his initial attempt at opera, The Sapphire Necklace (1863–64) with a libretto by Henry F. Chorley, was not produced and, apart from the Overture and two songs published separately, is now lost.

His first surviving opera, Cox and Box (1866), was written for a private performance. It then received charity performances in London and Manchester, and was later produced at the Gallery of Illustration, where it ran for an extraordinary 264 performances. His soon to be partner, W. S. Gilbert, writing in Fun magazine, announced the score as superior to F. C. Burnand's libretto.

In 1867 Sullivan and Burnand were commissioned by Thomas German Reed for a two-act opera, The Contrabandista (revised and expanded as The Chieftain in 1894), but it was a much more modest success.

Sullivan wrote a group of seven part songs in 1868, the best-known of which is "The Long Day Closes". His last major work of the 1860s was a short oratorio, The Prodigal Son, which premiered in Worcester Cathedral as part of the 1869 Three Choirs Festival to much praise.

The Overture di Ballo, Sullivan's most enduring work, was composed for the Birmingham Festival in 1870.

1871 was a busy year. Sullivan published his only song cycle, The Window; or, The Songs of the Wrens, to words by Tennyson, and wrote the first of a series of suites of incidental music for West End productions of Shakespeare plays. Later in the year he composed a dramatic cantata, On Shore and Sea, for the opening of the London International Exhibition, and the beautiful hymn Onward, Christian Soldiers, with words by Sabine Baring-Gould. The Salvation Army adopted it and it has become one of Britain's best loved hymns.

Gilbert & Sullivan – The Collaboration Begins

In 1871, John Hollingshead commissioned Gilbert to work with Sullivan on a holiday piece for Christmas, entitled Thespis, or The Gods Grown Old, at the Gaiety Theatre. It was a success and its run was extended beyond the length of the Gaiety's normal run. And that seemed to be that.

Gilbert and Sullivan now went their separate ways. Gilbert worked again with Clay on Happy Arcadia (1872), and with Alfred Cellier on Topsyturveydom (1874), as well as several farces, operetta libretti, extravaganzas, fairy comedies, adaptations from novels, translations from the French. In 1874, he published his last piece for Fun magazine ("Rosencrantz and Guildenstern"), almost three years after his last and then promptly resigned citing disapproval of the new owner's other publishing interests.

Sullivan was busy on large-scale works in the early 1870s with the Festival Te Deum (Crystal Palace, 1872); and the oratorio, The Light of the World (Birmingham Festival, 1873). He also wrote suites of incidental music for productions of The Merry Wives of Windsor at the Gaiety in 1874 and Henry VIII at the Theatre Royal, Manchester in 1877 as well as continuing composing hymns.

In 1873, Sullivan had also contributed songs to Burnand's Christmas "drawing room extravaganza", The Miller and His Man.

By 1875 conditions were right for Gilbert and Sullivan to work together again. Back in 1868, Gilbert had published a short comedic libretto in Fun magazine entitled "Trial by Jury: An Operetta". In 1873, Gilbert had arranged with theatrical manager and composer, Carl Rosa, to expand this work into a one-act libretto. It was arranged that Rosa's wife was to sing the role of the plaintiff. Tragically, Rosa's wife died in childbirth in 1874. Gilbert offered the libretto to Richard D'Oyly Carte, but Carte could not use the piece at that time.

The project seemed grounded. A few months later Carte, was managing the Royalty Theatre, needed a short piece to pair with Offenbach's La Périchole. Carte had previously conducted Sullivan's Cox and Box and remembering that Gilbert had suggested a libretto to him, he reunited Gilbert and Sullivan. The result was the one-act comic opera Trial by Jury. Starring Sullivan's brother Fred as the Learned Judge, it became a surprise hit, as well as earning lavish praise from the critics. It played for over 300 performances in its first few seasons.

A short time after Trial had opened Sullivan wrote The Zoo, another one-act comic opera, with a libretto by B. C. Stephenson. It did not perform well. Now the path was clear for Gilbert & Sullivan to reteam together in earnest and dominate light opera for the next 15 years.

Light opera was not considered of much worth by serious critics. Gilbert wanted greater respect for himself and his profession. At that time plays were not published in a form suitable for a "gentleman's library", they were in the main cheap and unattractive in their look designed mainly for use by actors rather than the home reader. Gilbert now arranged in late 1875 for the publishers Chatto and Windus to print a volume of his plays in a format designed to appeal to the general reader, with an attractive binding and clear type, containing Gilbert's most respectable plays, including his most serious works, and mischievously capped off with Trial by Jury.

After the success of Trial by Jury, there were discussions towards reviving Thespis, but Gilbert and Sullivan were not able to agree on terms with Carte and his backers. The score to Thespis was never published, and tragically most of the music is now lost.

Carte took some time to gather together funds for another opera, and in this gap the ever-busy Gilbert produced several works including Tom Cobb (1875), Eyes and No Eyes (1875), and Princess Toto (1876), his last and most ambitious work with Clay, a three-act comic opera with full orchestra. He also found time to write two serious works, Broken Hearts (1875) and Dan'l Druce, Blacksmith (1876) and his most successful comic play, Engaged (1877), which inspired Oscar Wilde's The Importance of Being Earnest.

It was only by 1877 that Carte finally assembled enough investors to form the Comedy Opera Company with a mandate to launch a series of original English comic operas, beginning with a third collaboration between Gilbert and Sullivan, The Sorcerer, in November 1877.

The Sorcerer (1877), ran for 178 performances, a success by the standards of the day, but H.M.S. Pinafore (1878), which followed it, turned Gilbert and Sullivan into an international phenomenon. The bright and cheerful music of Pinafore was composed during a time when Sullivan was in the middle of a health scare. He was in terrible pain from a kidney stone. H.M.S. Pinafore ran for 571 performances in London, the then-second-longest theatrical run in history, it also gave birth to and more than 150 unauthorised productions in America alone. Although this increased the reach of their reputations it added nothing to their profits.

It was noted in the Times review of H.M.S. Pinafore that the opera was an early attempt at the establishment of a "national musical stage" ... free from risqué French "improprieties" and without the "aid" of Italian and German musical models.

As the profits rolled in came acrimony among the investors who felt the shares were unequal. One night the other Comedy Opera Company partners hired thugs to storm the theatre to steal the sets and costumes in order that they could mount a rival production. This was beaten off by stagehands and others at the theatre loyal to Carte. Carte was to now continue as sole impresario of the newly renamed D'Oyly Carte Opera Company.

For the next decade, the Savoy Operas were Gilbert's principal activity. The successful comic operas with Sullivan continued to appear every year or two, several of them being among the longest-running productions of the musical stage. After Pinafore came The Pirates of Penzance (1879), Patience (1881), Iolanthe (1882), Princess Ida (1884 and based on Gilbert's earlier farce, The Princess), The Mikado (1885), Ruddigore (1887), The Yeomen of the Guard (1888), and The Gondoliers (1889). Gilbert not only directed and oversaw all aspects of production, but he designed the costumes himself for Patience, Iolanthe, Princess Ida, and Ruddigore. He insisted on precise and authentic sets and costumes, which provided a foundation to ground and focus his absurd characters and situations.

In 1878, Gilbert realised a lifelong dream to play Harlequin, which he did at the Gaiety Theatre in an amateur charity production of The Forty Thieves, written partly by himself. Gilbert trained for Harlequin's stylised dancing with his friend John D'Auban, who had arranged the dances for some of his plays and would choreograph most of the Gilbert and Sullivan operas. Producer John Hollingshead later remembered, "the gem of the performance was the grimly earnest and determined Harlequin of W. S. Gilbert. It gave me an idea of what Oliver Cromwell would have made of the character."

In 1879, Sullivan suggested to a reporter from The New York Times the secret of his success with Gilbert: "His ideas are as suggestive for music as they are quaint and laughable. His numbers ... always give me musical ideas."

During this time, Gilbert and Sullivan also collaborated on one other major work. In 1880, Sullivan was appointed director of the triennial Leeds Music Festival. For his first festival he was commissioned to write a sacred choral work. He chose Henry Hart Milman's 1822 dramatic poem based on the life and death of Saint Margaret the Virgin for its basis. It premiered at the Leeds music festival in October 1880. Gilbert arranged the original epic poem by Henry Hart Milman into a libretto suitable for the music.

Carte opened the next Gilbert and Sullivan piece, Patience, in April 1881 at London's Opera Comique, where their past three operas had played. In October, Patience transferred to the new, larger, state-of-the-art (it was the first theatre to be lit entirely with electricity) Savoy Theatre, built with the profits of the previous Gilbert and Sullivan works.

From now on all of the partnership's collaborations were produced at the Savoy. The first to actually premiere here was Iolanthe in 1882, it was their fourth hit in a row.

Cracks were beginning to surface between the partners. Sullivan, despite the financial security, began to view his work with Gilbert as beneath his skills, as well as being repetitious. After Iolanthe, Sullivan had not intended to write a new work with Gilbert, but when his broker went bankrupt in late 1882 he suffered serious financial loss. Needs must and Sullivan buckled down to continue writing Savoy operas. In February 1883, he and Gilbert signed a five-year agreement with Carte, requiring them to produce a new comic opera on six months' notice.

The ever watchful Gilbert had the previous year installed a telephone in his home and another at the prompt desk at the Savoy Theatre, so that he could listen in on performances and rehearsals from his home study. Gilbert had referred to the new technology in Pinafore in 1878, only two years after the device was invented and before London even had telephones.

Better news arrived for Sullivan on May 22nd, 1883, when he was knighted by Queen Victoria for his "services ... rendered to the promotion of the art of music" in Britain. The musical establishment, and many critics, believed that this would put an end to his career as a composer of comic opera – that a musical knight should not stoop below oratorio or grand opera. But Sullivan having just signed the five-year agreement and the financial security that gave him could no nothing to change course now.

The next opera, Princess Ida in 1884, which was the duo's only three-act, blank verse work, stuttered. Its run was much shorter. Sullivan's score was praised but with box office receipts lagging in March 1884, Carte gave the six months' notice, under the partnership contract, requiring a new opera.

Sullivan's friend, composer Frederic Clay, had suffered a serious stroke in early December 1883 that ended his career at only 45 years of age. Sullivan, with his own longstanding kidney problems, and his desire to devote himself to more serious music, replied to Carte, "It is impossible for me to do another piece of the character of those already written by Gilbert and myself."

Gilbert however was already at work on it. His idea revolved around a plot in which people fell in love against their wills after taking a magic lozenge. Sullivan was unequoviacal in his response. On April 1st, 1884 he wrote that he had "come to the end of my tether with the operas. I have been continually keeping down the music in order that not one syllable should be lost.... I should like to set a story of human interest & probability where the humorous words would come in a humorous not serious situation, & where, if the situation were a tender or dramatic one the words would be of similar character."

There was now a lengthy exchange of correspondence in which Sullivan called Gilbert's plot sketch (particularly the "lozenge" element) unacceptably mechanical, and too similar in both its grotesque "elements of topsyturveydom" and in actual plot to their earlier work, especially The Sorcerer, and requested, time and again, that a new subject be found.

This impasse was finally resolved on May 8th when Gilbert proposed a plot that would be their most successful: The Mikado (1885). It was to run for a staggering 672 performances.

In 1886, Sullivan composed his last large-scale choral work of the decade. It was a cantata for the Leeds Festival, The Golden Legend, based on Longfellow's poem of the same name. Apart from the comic operas, this proved to be Sullivan's best received full-length work. It was given hundreds of performances during his lifetime alone.

Ruddigore followed The Mikado in 1887. It was profitable, but its nine-month run was deemed to be disappointing compared with the earlier Savoy operas.

Gilbert was always keen to use a good idea again and proposed for their next piece another version of the magic lozenge plot. It was immediately rejected by Sullivan. Gilbert finally proposed a quite serious opera, to which Sullivan was in agreement. Although not a grand opera, The Yeomen of the Guard (1888) gave him the opportunity to compose his most ambitious stage work to date. In 1885, Sullivan had told an interviewer, ""The opera of the future is a compromise (among the French, German and Italian schools) – a sort of eclectic school, a selection of the merits of each one. I myself will make an attempt to produce a grand opera of this new school. ... Yes, it will be an historical work, and it is the dream of my life."

After The Yeomen of the Guard opened, Sullivan turned once again to Shakespeare and composed incidental music for Henry Irving's production of Macbeth (1888).

Sullivan wished to produce further serious works with Gilbert. He had collaborated with no other librettist since 1875. Gilbert felt the reaction to The Yeomen of the Guard had "not been so convincing as to warrant us in assuming that the public want something more earnest still." Gilbert countered by proposing that Sullivan should go ahead with his plan to write a grand opera, as well as comic works for the Savoy. Sullivan was not immediately persuaded. He replied, "I have lost the liking for writing comic opera, and entertain very grave doubts as to my power of doing it."

Nevertheless, Sullivan soon commissioned a grand opera libretto from Julian Sturgis (the recommendation came from Gilbert), while suggesting to Gilbert that he revive an old idea for an opera set in colourful Venice. The comic opera was completed first in 1889. The Gondoliers has been described as a pinnacle of Sullivan's achievement. It was to be the last great Gilbert and Sullivan success.

In April 1890, during the run of The Gondoliers, Gilbert objected to Carte's financial accounts which included a charge to the partnership for the cost of new carpeting for the Savoy Theatre lobby. Gilbert believed that this was a maintenance expense that should be charged to Carte alone. Carte who was building a new theatre to present Sullivan's forthcoming grand opera was adamant that it was legitimate. Sullivan sided with Carte, even going so far as to testify erroneously as to certain old debts.

The partners were in fundamental disagreement and the relationship was for all intents and purposes ruptured.

Gilbert took legal action against Carte and Sullivan and refused to write a word more for the Savoy. Sullivan wrote to Gilbert in September 1890 that he was "physically and mentally ill over this wretched business. I have not yet got over the shock of seeing our names coupled ... in hostile antagonism over a few miserable pounds".

From Gilbert's point of view Carte had either made a series of serious blunders in the accounts, or deliberately attempted to swindle his partners.

Gilbert wrote to Sullivan on May 28th, 1891, a year after the end of the "Quarrel", that Carte had admitted "an unintentional overcharge of nearly £1,000 in the electric lighting accounts alone." It seemed to illustrate Gilbert's point.

Work beckoned for Gilbert and he got on with it. He wrote The Mountebanks with Alfred Cellier and then a flop Haste to the Wedding with George Grossmith. Sullivan wrote Haddon Hall with Sydney Grundy.

In the Courts Gilbert prevailed in the lawsuit and felt vindicated. Although there was acrimony and bitterness between them the partnership had been so profitable that, after the financial failure of the Royal English Opera House, Carte and his wife sought to reunite the author and composer.

In 1891, after numerous failed attempts at a reconciliation, Tom Chappell, the music publisher who printed the Gilbert and Sullivan operas, stepped in to mediate between his two most profitable artists, and within two weeks, against the odds, had succeeded. The result was to be two more operas: Utopia, Limited (1893) and The Grand Duke (1896).

A third was almost achieved when Gilbert offered a third libretto to Sullivan (His Excellency, 1894), but his insistence on casting Nancy McIntosh, his protegée from Utopia, led to Sullivan's refusal.

Utopia, was only a modest success, and The Grand Duke, in which a theatrical troupe, by means of a "statutory duel" and a conspiracy, takes political control of a grand duchy, was a failure.

The partnership now ended for good.

Graciously Gilbert would late write, "... Savoy opera was snuffed out by the deplorable death of my distinguished collaborator, Sir Arthur Sullivan. When that event occurred, I saw no one with whom I felt that I could work with satisfaction and success, and so I discontinued to write libretti."

WS Gilbert – Life After the Partnership

In 1889 Gilbert financed the building of the Garrick Theatre. The following year the Gilberts moved to Grim's Dyke in Harrow. In 1891, Gilbert was appointed Justice of the Peace for Middlesex. After casting Nancy McIntosh in Utopia, Limited, he and Lady Gilbert developed an affection for her, and she eventually gained the status of an unofficially adopted daughter, moving to Grim's Dyke to live with them. She continued living there, even after Gilbert's death, until Lady Gilbert's death in 1936.

Although Gilbert announced a retirement from the theatre after the poor initial run of his last work with Sullivan, The Grand Duke (1896) and the poor reception of his 1897 play The Fortune Hunter, he produced at least three more plays over the last dozen years of his life, including an unsuccessful opera, Fallen Fairies (1909), with Edward German.

Gilbert, as we know was very keen on keeping his plays in the shape they were originally intended and continued to supervise the various revivals of his works by the D'Oyly Carte Opera Company, including its London Repertory seasons in 1906–09.

The last play he wrote, The Hooligan, produced just four months before his death, is a study of a young condemned thug in a prison cell. Gilbert shows sympathy for his protagonist, the son of a thief who, brought up among thieves, kills his girlfriend.

This grim, yet powerful piece, became one of Gilbert's most successful serious dramas, and it is easy to see why many thought he was developing a new style only for death to rob us of what would surely be a fascinating journey.

In these last years, Gilbert wrote children's book versions of H.M.S. Pinafore and The Mikado giving, in some cases, backstory that is not found in the librettos.

Official recognition for him came on July 15th, 1907 with his knighthood in recognition of his contributions to drama. Gilbert was the first British writer ever to receive a knighthood for his plays alone—earlier dramatist knights were knighted for political and other services.

On May 29th, 1911, Gilbert was about to give a swimming lesson to Winifred Isabel Emery and 17-year-old Ruby Preece in the lake of his home, Grim's Dyke, when Preece lost her footing and called for help. Gilbert dived in to save her but suffered a heart attack in the middle of the lake and died.

William Schwenck was cremated at Golders Green and his ashes buried at the Church of St. John the Evangelist, Stanmore. The inscription on Gilbert's memorial on the south wall of the Thames Embankment in London reads: "His Foe was Folly, and his Weapon Wit".

George Grossmith wrote to The Daily Telegraph that, although Gilbert had been described as an autocrat at rehearsals, "That was really only his manner when he was playing the part of stage director at rehearsals. As a matter of fact, he was a generous, kind true gentleman, and I use the word in the purest and original sense."

Gilbert's legacy, aside from building the Garrick Theatre are the canon of Savoy Operas and other works that are either still being performed or in print all these years later. He has made a lasting and defining influence on both the American and British musical theatre. The innovations in content and form of the works that he and Sullivan developed, and in Gilbert's theories of acting and stage direction, directly influenced the development of the modern musical throughout the 20th century. Gilbert's lyrics use punning, as well as complex internal and two and three-syllable rhyme schemes, and served as a model for such 20th century Broadway lyricists as P.G. Wodehouse, Cole Porter, Ira Gershwin, and Lorenz Hart.

Gilbert's influence on the English language has also been marked, with well-known phrases such as "A policeman's lot is not a happy one", "short, sharp shock", "What never? Well, hardly ever!", and "let the punishment fit the crime" arising from his pen.

Arthur Sullivan – Life After the Partnership

Sullivan's only grand opera, Ivanhoe, based on Walter Scott's novel, opened at Carte's new Royal English Opera House on January 31st, 1891. Sullivan completed the score too late to meet Carte's planned production date, and costs had overrun to such an extent that Carte insisted on a contractual penalty of £3,000 for the delay. However, when it opened it ran 155 consecutive performances, a wonderful run for a serious opera, and garnered good reviews. Afterwards, Carte was unable to fill the new opera house with other productions, and, unfairly, Ivanhoe was blamed for the failure of the opera house.

Later in 1891, New York beckoned for Sullivan and his music for Tennyson's The Foresters, which ran at Daly's Theatre in New York in 1892, but failed in London the following year.

Sullivan returned to comic opera, but needed a new collaborator. His next piece was Haddon Hall in 1892, with a libretto by Sydney Grundy based somewhat loosely on the elopement of Dorothy Vernon with John Manners. Although still comic, the tone and style of the work was more serious and romantic than the operas with Gilbert. It nonetheless enjoyed a run of 204 performances, and earned critical praise.

In 1894 Sullivan teamed up again with F. C. Burnand for The Chieftain, a heavily-reworked version of their earlier two-act opera, The Contrabandista, alas it failed.

The following year Sullivan provided incidental music for the Lyceum, this time for J. Comyns Carr's King Arthur.

As we know Gilbert and Sullivan did reunite for The Grand Duke in 1896. But it failed and they never worked together again. This did not affect the constant revival of their earlier operas at the Savoy.

In May 1897, Sullivan's full-length ballet, Victoria and Merrie England, opened at the Alhambra Theatre in celebration of the Queen's Diamond Jubilee. The work's seven scenes celebrate English history and culture, with the Victorian period as the grand finale. It ran for six months which was a great achievement. Following this was The Beauty Stone in 1898, with a libretto by Arthur Wing Pinero and J. Comyns Carr. Based on mediaeval morality plays the opera was a critical failure and, on the whole, a commercial failure running for only seven weeks.

Success came in 1899, to benefit "the wives and children of soldiers and sailors" on active service in the Boer War, when Sullivan composed the music of a jingoistic song, "The Absent-Minded Beggar", to a text by Rudyard Kipling. It was a sensation and raised a staggering £250,000 from performances and the sale of sheet music and other merchandise. Later that year he returned to his comic roots with In The Rose of Persia, with a libretto by Basil Hood overlapping a setting of exotic Arabian Nights with plot elements of The Mikado. It was well received, and, apart from those with Gilbert, was his most successful full-length collaboration. Another opera with Hood, The Emerald Isle, quickly went into preparation, but sadly Sullivan died before it completion.

On November 22nd, 1900 Arthur Seymour Sullivan died of heart failure, following an attack of bronchitis, at his flat in London. The unfinished opera, The Emerald Isle, was completed by Edward German and premiered in 1901. His Te Deum Laudamus, written to commemorate the end of the Boer War, was performed posthumously.

Sullivan wished to be buried in Brompton Cemetery with his parents and brother, but by order of the Queen he was buried in St. Paul's Cathedral. In addition to his knighthood, honours awarded to Sullivan in his lifetime included Doctor in Music, honoris causa, by the universities of Cambridge (1876) and Oxford (1879); Chevalier, Légion d'honneur, France (1878); The Order of the Medjidieh conferred by the Sultan of Turkey (1888); and appointment as a Member of the Fourth Class of the Royal Victorian Order (MVO) in 1897.

In all, Sullivan's artistic output included 23 operas, 13 major orchestral works, eight choral works and oratorios, two ballets, one song cycle, incidental music to several plays, numerous hymns and other church pieces, and a large body of songs, parlour ballads, part songs, carols, and piano and chamber pieces.

Although Sullivan had several long term affairs and was also known to have a roving eye that led him to frequent liaisons with many other women he never married.

Rachel Scott Russell was the first of his great loves. Her parents' disapproval meant they met secretly but by 1868, Sullivan was enmeshed in a simultaneous and secret affair with Rachel's sister Louise. Both relationships had ceased by early 1869.

Sullivan's affair with the American socialite, Fanny Ronalds, a woman three years his senior, who had two children began when they met in Paris around 1867. The affair began in earnest soon after she moved to London in 1871. Despite his wandering ways she was a constant companion up to the time of Sullivan's death, but around 1889 or 1890, the sexual relationship seems to have ended.

In 1896, the 54-year-old Sullivan proposed marriage to 22-year-old Violet Beddington but she refused.

The favourite playgrounds for Sullivan were Paris and the south of France, with friends ranging from European royalty to Claude Debussy, and where the casinos enabled him to indulge his passion for gambling.

Sullivan enjoyed playing tennis although, according to George Grossmith, "I have seen some bad lawn-tennis players in my time, but I never saw anyone so bad as Arthur Sullivan".

He was devoted to his parents, particularly his mother, until her death in 1882. Henry Lytton wrote, "I believe there was never a more affectionate tie than that which existed between Sullivan and his mother, a very witty old lady, and one who took an exceptional pride in her son's accomplishments.

Sullivan once explained his method of working; "I don't use the piano in composition – that would limit me terribly". Sullivan explained that he did not wait for inspiration, but had "to dig for it. ... I decide on the rhythm before I come to the question of melody. ... I mark out the metre in dots and dashes, and not until I have quite settled on the rhythm do I proceed to actual notation."

In composing the Savoy operas, Sullivan wrote the vocal lines of the musical numbers first, and these were given to the actors. He, or an assistant, improvised a piano accompaniment at the early rehearsals; he wrote the orchestrations later, after he had seen what Gilbert's stage business would be. He left the overtures until last and often delegated their composition, based on his outlines, to his assistants, often adding his suggestions or corrections. Those Sullivan wrote himself include Thespis, Iolanthe, Princess Ida, The Yeomen of the Guard, The Gondoliers, The Grand Duke and probably Utopia Limited. Most of the overtures are structured as a potpourri of tunes from the operas in three sections: fast, slow and fast. The overtures from the Gilbert and Sullivan operas remain popular. Sullivan invariably conducted the operas on their opening nights.

In general, Sullivan preferred to write in major keys. In the Savoy operas less than 5% of the numbers are in a minor key and even in his serious works the major prevails. Sullivan was happy on occasion to use chords traditionally considered technically incorrect. When reproached for using consecutive fifths in Cox and Box, he replied "if 5ths turn up it doesn't matter, so long as there is no offence to the ear."

Sullivan's orchestra for the Savoy Operas was typical of any other pit orchestra of his era: 2 flutes (+ piccolo), oboe, 2 clarinets, bassoon, 2 horns, 2 cornets, 2 trombones, timpani, percussion and strings. According to Geoffrey Toye, the number of players in the Savoy orchestra was originally 31. Sullivan argued hard for an increase in the pit orchestra's size, and starting with The Yeomen of the Guard, the orchestra was augmented with a second bassoon and a bass trombone. Sullivan generally orchestrated each score at almost the last moment, noting that the accompaniment for an opera had to wait until he saw the staging, so that he could judge how heavily or lightly to orchestrate each part of the music. For his large-scale orchestral pieces, Sullivan added a second oboe part, sometimes double bassoon and bass clarinet, more horns, trumpets, tuba, and sometimes an organ and/or a harp. Many of these pieces used very large orchestras.

Sullivan's critical reputation has undergone extreme changes since he first came to prominence in the 1860s. At first, critics were struck by his potential, and he was hailed as the long-awaited great English composer. His incidental music to The Tempest received an acclaimed premiere at the Crystal Palace just before Sullivan's 20th birthday in April 1862. The Athenaeum wrote:

When Sullivan turned to comic opera with Gilbert, the serious critics began to express disapproval. Peter Gammond writes of "misapprehensions and prejudices, delivered to our door by the Victorian firm Musical Snobs Ltd. ... frivolity and high spirits were sincerely seen as elements that could not be exhibited by anyone who was to be admitted to the sanctified society of Art." As early as 1877 The Figaro wrote that Sullivan "has all the ability to make him a great composer, but he wilfully throws his opportunity away. ... He possesses all the natural ability to have given us an English opera, and, instead, he affords us a little more-or-less excellent fooling." Few critics denied the excellence of Sullivan's theatre scores. The Theatre wrote that "Iolanthe sustains Dr Sullivan's reputation as the most spontaneous, fertile, and scholarly composer of comic opera this country has ever produced." However, comic opera, no matter how skilfully crafted, was viewed as an intrinsically lower form of art than oratorio. The Athenaeum's review of The Martyr of Antioch declared: "It is an advantage to have the composer of H.M.S. Pinafore occupying himself with a worthier form of art."

Although the more solemn members of the musical establishment could not forgive Sullivan for writing music that was both comic and accessible, he was, nevertheless, "the nation's de facto composer laureate".

Gilbert & Sullivan – A Concise Bibliography

The Collaborative Pieces

All of these operas are full-length two-act works, except for Trial by Jury, which is in one act, and Princess Ida, which is three acts.

Thespis (1871)
Trial by Jury (1875)
The Sorcerer (1877)
H.M.S. Pinafore (1878)
The Pirates of Penzance (1879)
Patience (1881)
Iolanthe (1882)
Princess Ida (1884)
The Mikado (1885)
Ruddigore (1887)
The Yeomen of the Guard (1888)
The Gondoliers (1889)
Utopia, Limited (1893)
The Grand Duke (1896)

W.S. Gilbert – his Other Works

Poetry
The Bab Ballads, a collection of comic verse published roughly between 1865 and 1871
Songs of a Savoyard, London, 1890, a collection of Gilbert's song lyrics.

Short Stories
Foggerty's Fairy & Other Tales, a collection of short stories and essays, mainly from before 1874.

Some other short stories but not in the above appear here:-

Belgravia, Vol. 2 (1867). "From St. Paul's to Piccadilly," pp. 67–74
Fun, Vol. 1 new series (1865-1866) (several contributions by Gilbert; near end of volume)
Fun Christmas Number 1865, ("The Astounding Adventure of Wheeler J. Calamity,")
London Society, Vol. 13 (1868) (three "Thumbnail Sketches" by Gilbert)
On the Cards: Routledge's Christmas Annual (1867) ("Diamonds," and "The Converted Clown,")

Other Books
The Pinafore Picture Book, 1908, retelling the story of H.M.S. Pinafore for children, in prose narrative
The Story of The Mikado, 1921, a similar retelling of The Mikado for children

Plays and Musical Stage Works
Selected stage works that were important to Gilbert's career or were otherwise notable, in chronological order, excluding those listed under other headings below:

Dulcamara, or the Little Duck and the Great Quack (1866)
La Vivandière (1867)
Harlequin Cock Robin and Jenny Wren (1867), a Christmas pantomime.
The Merry Zingara (1868)
Robert the Devil (1868), it opened the Gaiety Theatre, London and ran in the provinces for 3 years.
The Pretty Druidess (1869), a parody of Norma – the last of Gilbert's five "operatic burlesques"
An Old Score (1869) (rewritten as "Quits!" in 1872) Gilbert's first full-length comedy.
The Princess (1870). Musical farce; the precursor to Princess Ida.
The Palace of Truth (1870).
Creatures of Impulse (1871), music by Alberto Randegger. From Gilberts story "A Strange Old Lady".
Pygmalion and Galatea (1871).
Randall's Thumb (1871). A comedy that opened the Royal Court Theatre.
The Wicked World (1873).
The Happy Land (1873). This work was briefly banned for its sharp satire of government ministers.
The Realm of Joy (1873).
The Wedding March (1873) a farce adapted from Un Chapeau de Paille d'Italie.
Rosencrantz & Guildenstern (published 1874, performed 1891). Gilbert's burlesque of Hamlet.
Charity (1874). Concerns Victorian attitudes towards sex outside of marriage.
Sweethearts (1874).

Tom Cobb (1875).
Broken Hearts (1875). The last of Gilbert's "fairy comedies", this was one of Gilbert's favourite plays.
Dan'l Druce, Blacksmith (1876).
Engaged (1877).
The Ne'er-do-Weel (1878); rewritten as "The Vagabond" after a few weeks.
The Forty Thieves (1878). Co-written with three other writers, WSG played Harlequin.
Gretchen (1879)
Foggerty's Fairy (1881)
Brantinghame Hall (1888) Gilbert's biggest flop, it sent producer Rutland Barrington into bankruptcy.
The Fortune Hunter (1897). Its reception provoked WSG to announce retiring from writing for the stage.
The Fairy's Dilemma (1904).
The Hooligan (1911).

German Reed Entertainments
Gilbert wrote six one-act musical entertainments for the German Reeds between 1869 and 1875. They were successful in their own right and also helped form Gilbert's mature style as a dramatist.

No Cards (1869)
Ages Ago (1869). Gilbert's first collaboration with Frederic Clay, ran for 350 performances.
Our Island Home (1870)
A Sensation Novel (1871)
Happy Arcadia (1872)
Eyes and No Eyes (1875)

Early Comic Operas
The Gentleman in Black (1870; music by Frederic Clay). The score is lost.
Les Brigands (1871), an English adaptation of Jacques Offenbach's operetta.
Topsyturveydom (1874; music by Alfred Cellier). The score is lost.
Princess Toto (1876; music by Frederic Clay). A three-act opera.

Later Operas (Without Sullivan)
Though not as popular as the works with Arthur Sullivan, a few of Gilbert's later works arguably have stronger plots than the last two Gilbert and Sullivan operas.

The Mountebanks (1892; music; Alfred Cellier). This is the "lozenge plot" that Sullivan declined to set on several occasions.
Haste to the Wedding (1892; music; George Grossmith). An unsuccessful adaptation of The Wedding March.
His Excellency (1894; music; Osmond Carr). Gilbert felt that if Sullivan had set it, the piece would have been "another Mikado".
Fallen Fairies (1909; music by Edward German). Gilbert's last opera, which was a failure.

Parlour Ballads
The Yarn of the Nancy Bell, with music by Alfred Plumpton. One of the Bab Ballads. 1869.

Thady O'Flynn, with music by James L. Molloy. 1868. From No Cards.
Would You Know that Maiden Fair, with music by Frederic Clay. From Ages Ago. c. 1869.
Corisande, with music by James L. Molloy. 1870.
Eily's Reason, with music by James L. Molloy. 1871.
Three songs from A Sensation Novel: "The Detective's Song", "The Tyrannical Bridegroom", and "The Jewel". 1871
The Distant Shore, with music by Arthur Sullivan. 1874.
The Love that Loves me Not, with music by Arthur Sullivan. 1875.
Sweethearts, with music by Arthur Sullivan. 1875.
Let Me Stay, with music by Walter Maynard. 1875.

Arthur Sullivan – His Other Works

Operas
The Sapphire Necklace (ca. 1863; unperformed)
Cox and Box (1866)
The Contrabandista (1867)
The Zoo (1875)
Ivanhoe (1891)
Haddon Hall (1892)
The Chieftain (1894)
The Beauty Stone (1898)
The Rose of Persia (1899)
The Emerald Isle (1901; completed by Edward German)

Incidental Music to Plays
The Tempest (1861)
The Merchant of Venice (1871)
The Merry Wives of Windsor (1874)
Henry VIII (1877)
Macbeth (1888)
Tennyson's The Foresters (1892)
J. Comyns Carr's King Arthur for Henry Irving (1895)

Sheet Music

Ballets and Song Cycle
L'Île Enchantée (1864 ballet)
Victoria and Merrie England (1897 ballet)
The Window; or, The Song of the Wrens (1871 song cycle)

Choral Works with Orchestra
The Masque at Kenilworth (1864)

The Prodigal Son (Sullivan) (1869)
On Shore and Sea (1871)
Festival Te Deum (1872)
The Light of the World (Sullivan) (1873)
The Martyr of Antioch (1880)
Ode for the Opening of the Colonial and Indian Exhibition (1886)
The Golden Legend (1886)
Ode for the Laying of the Foundation Stone of The Imperial Institute (1887)
Te Deum Laudamus (1902; performed posthumously)

Orchestral Works
Overture in D (1858; now lost)
Overture The Feast of Roses (1860; now lost)
Procession March (1863)
Princess of Wales's March (1863)
Symphony in E, "Irish" (1866)
Overture in C, "In Memoriam" (1866)
Concerto for Cello and Orchestra (1866)
Overture Marmion (1867)
Overture di Ballo (1870)
Imperial March (1893)
The Absent-Minded Beggar March (1899)

Other Works

Songs & Parlour Ballads
Absent-minded Beggar (Rudyard Kipling) 1899
Arabian Love Song (Percy Bysshe Shelley) 1866
Ay de mi, My Bird (George Eliot)1874
Bid me at least Goodbye (Sydney Grundy) 1894
Birds in the Night (Lionel H. Lewin) 1869
Bride from the North (Henry F. Chorley) 1863
Care is all Fiddle-dee-dee (F. C. Burnand) 1874
Chorister, The (Fred. E. Weatherly) 1876
Christmas Bells at Sea (C. L. Kenney) 1875
County Guy (Walter Scott) 1867
Distant Shore, The (W. S. Gilbert) 1874
Dove Song (William Brough) 1869
E tu nol sai - see You Sleep (G. Mazzucato) 1889
Edward Gray (Alfred Tennyson)(1880
Ever (Mrs Bloomfield Moore) 1887
First Departure - see The Chorister (Rev. E. Munroe) 1874
Give (Adelaide Anne Procter) 1867
Golden Days (Lionel H. Lewin)1872
Guinevere! (Lionel H. Lewin) 1872
I Heard the Nightingale (Rev. C. H. Townsend) 1863

I Wish to Tune my Quiv'ring Lyre (Anacreon; trans. Lord Byron) 1868
I Would I were a King (Victor Hugo; trans. A. Cockburn) 1878
Ich möchte hinaus es jauchzen (A. Corrodi) 1859
If Doughty Deeds (Robert Graham of Gartmore) 1866
In the Summers Long Ago (J. P. Douglas) 1867
Let Me Dream Again (B. C. Stephenson) 1875
Lied, mit Thränen halbgeschrieben (Eichendorff) 1861
Life that Lives for You (Lionel H. Lewin) 1870
Little Darling Sleep Again (Cradle Song) (anon) 1874
Living Poems (H. W. Longfellow) 1874
Longing for Home (Jean Ingelow) 1904
Looking Back (Louisa Gray)1870
Looking Forward (Louisa Gray) 1873
Lost Chord, The (Adelaide Anne Procter) 1877
Love that Loves Me Not, The (W. S. Gilbert) 1875
Maiden's Story, The (Emma Embury) 1867
Marquis de Mincepie, The (F. C. Burnand) 1874
Mary Morison (Robert Burns) 1874
Moon in Silent Brightness, The (Bishop Reginald Heber) 1868
Mother's Dream, The (Rev. W. Barnes) 1868
My Dear and Only Love (Marquis of Montrose) 1874
My Dearest Heart (anon) 1874
My Heart is like a Silent Lute (Benjamin Disraeli) 1904
My Love - see "There Sits a Bird in Yonder Tree
My Love Beyond the Sea - see "In the Summers Long Ago"
None but I Can Say (Lionel H. Lewin)1872
O Fair Dove, O Fond Dove (Jean Ingelow) 1868
O Israel (Hosea) 1855
O Mistress Mine (William Shakespeare) 1866
O Swallow, Swallow (Alfred Tennyson) 1900
Oh Sweet and Fair (A. F. C. K.) 1868
Oh! bella mia - see "Oh! Ma Charmante"
Oh! Ma Charmante (Victor Hugo) 1872
Old Love Letters (S. K. Cowen) 1879
Once Again (Lionel H. Lewin) 1872
Orpheus with his Lute (William Shakespeare) 1866
River, The (anon) 1875
Roads Should Blossom, The (anon) 1864
Rosalind (William Shakespeare) 1866
Sad Memories (C. J. Rowe) 1869
Sailor's Grave, The (H. F. Lyte) 1872
St. Agnes' Eve (Alfred Tennyson) 1879
Shadow, A. (Adelaide Anne Procter) 1886
She is not Fair to Outward View (Hartley Coleridge) 1866
Sigh no More, Ladies (William Shakespeare) 1866
Sleep My Love, Sleep (R. Whyte Melville) 1874
Snow Lies White, The (Jean Ingelow) 1868
Sometimes (Lady Lindsay of Balcarres) 1877

Sweet Day So Cool (George Herbert) 1864
Sweet Dreamer - see "Oh! Ma Charmante"
Sweethearts (W. S. Gilbert) 1875
Tears, Idle Tears (Alfred Tennyson) 1900
Tender and True (Dinah Maria Mulock) 1874
There Sits a Bird on Yonder TreeRev. (C. H. Barham) 1873
Thou art Lost to Me (anon) 1865
Thou art Weary (Adelaide Anne Procter) 1874
Thou'rt Passing Hence (Felicia Hemans) 1875
To One in Paradise (Edgar Allan Poe) 1904
Troubadour, The (Walter Scott) 1869
Village Chimes, The (C. J. Rowe) 1870
Weary Lot is Thine, Fair Maid, A (Walter Scott) 1866
We've Ploughed our Land (anon)1875
When Thou Art Near (W. J. Stewart) 1877
White Plume, The - see "The Bride from the North"
Will He Come? (Adelaide A. Procter) 1865
Willow Song, The (William Shakespeare)1866
You Sleep (B. C. Stephenson) 1889

Hymns (Title & First Line)
Adoro Te - Saviour, again to Thy dear name we raise (Arranger)
All This Night - All this night bright angels sing
Angel Voices - Angel voices, ever singing
Audite Audientes me - I heard the voice of Jesus say
Bethlehem - While shepherd's watched their flocks (Arranger)
Bishopgarth - O King of Kings, Whose reign of old
Bolwell - Thou to whom the sick and dying
Carrow - My God, I thank Thee Who has made
Chapel Royal - O love that wilt not let me go
Christus - Show me not only Jesus dying
Clarence - Winter reigneth o'er the land
Coena Domini - Draw nigh, and take the body of the Lord
Come Unto Me - Come unto Me, ye weary (Arranger)
Constance - I've found a Friend; oh, such a Friend
Coronae - Crown Him, with many crowns
Courage, Brother - Courage, brother, do not stumble
Dominion Hymn - God bless our wide dominion
Dulce Sonans - Angel voices, ever singing
Ecclesia - The church has waited long
Ellers - Saviour, again to Thy dear name we raise (Arranger)
Evelyn - In the hour of my distress
Ever Faithful - Let us with a gladsome mind
Fatherland (St. Edmund) - I'm but a stranger here
Formosa (Falfield) - Love Divine, all love excelling
Fortunatus - Welcome, happy morning!
Golden Sheaves - To Thee, O Lord, our hearts we raise

Hanford - Jesu, my Saviour, look on me
Heber (Gennesareth) - When through the torn sail
Holy City - Sing Alleluia forth in duteous praise
Hushed was the Evening Hymn - Hushed was the evening hymn
Hymn of the Homeland - The homeland, the homeland
Lacrymae - Lord, in this Thy mercy's day
Leominster - A few more years shall roll (Arranger)
Light - Holy Spirit! Come in might! (Arranger)
Litany (1) - Jesu, life of those who die
Litany (2) - Jesu, we are far away
Long Home, The - Tender Shepherd, Thou hast still'd
Lux eoi - All is bright and cheeful round us
Lux in Tenebris - Lead, kindly Light
Lux Mundi - O Jesu, Thou art standing
Marlborough - O Strength and Stay, upholding all creation (Arranger)
Mount Zion - Rock of Ages, cleft for me
Nearer Home - For ever with the Lord (Arranger)
Noel - It came upon the midnight clear (Arranger)
Old 137th - Great King of nations, hear our prayer (Arranger)
Paradise - O Paradise!
Parting - With the sweet word of peace (Arranger)
Pilgrimage - From Egypt's bondage come
Promissio Patris - Our blest Redeemer, ere He breathed
Propior Deo - Nearer, my God, to Thee
Rest - Art thou weary, art thou languid
Resurrexit - Christ is risen!
Roseate Hues, The - The roseate hues of early dawn
Safe Home - Safe home, safe home in port
St. Ann - The Son of God goes forth to war (Arranger)
St. Francis - O Father, who hast created all
St. Gertrude - Onward, Christian soldiers
St. Kevin - Come, ye faithful, raise the strain
St. Lucian - Of Thy love some gracious token
St. Luke (St. Nathaniel) - God moves in a mysterious way
St. Mary Magdalene - Saviour, when in dust to Thee
St. Millicent - Let no tears to-day be shed
St. Patrick - He is gone - a cloud of light
St. Theresa - Brightly gleams our banner
Saints of God - The Saints of God, their conflict past.
Springtime - For all Thy love and goodness (Arranger)
Strain Upraise, The - The Strain upraise in joy and praise
Thou God of Love - Thou God of Love, beneath Thy sheltering wing
Ultor Omnipotens - God the all terrible! King who ordainest
Valete - Sweet Saviour, bless us 'ere we go
Veni, Creator - Come Holy Ghost, our souls inspire
Victoria - To mourn our dead we gather here

Part Songs

The term "Part Song" is more usually applied to one where the highest part carries the melody with the other voices supplying the accompanying harmonies.

Also included here are the soprano duet, The Sisters, and the trio Sullivan composed for the play Olivia by W. G. Wills, Morn, Happy Morn.

O Lady Dear (Madrigal) - Composed 1857, unpublished.
It was a Lover and his Lass - Words by Shakespeare. Performed at the Royal Academy of Music, 1857, unpublished.
Seaside Thoughts - Words by Bernard Bartram. Composed 1857. Published 1904.
The Last Night of the Year - Words by H. F. Chorley. Published 1863.
O Hush Thee, My Babie - Words by Walter Scott. Published 1867.
The Rainy Day - Words by H. W. Longfellow. Published 1867.
Evening - Words by Lord Houghton, after Goethe. Published 1868.
Parting Gleams - Words by Aubrey de Vere. Published 1868.
Echoes - Words by Thomas Moore. Published 1868.
The Long Day Closes - Words by H. F. Chorley. Published 1868.
Joy to the Victors - Words by Walter Scott. Published 1868
The Beleaguered - Words by H. F. Chorley. Published 1868.
It Came Upon the Midnight Clear - Words by E. H. Sears. Published 1871.
Lead, Kindly Light - Words by J. H. Newman. Published 1871.
Through Sorrows Path - Words by H. Kirke White. Published 1871.
Say, Watchman, What of the Night? - Words from Isaiah. Published 1871.
The Way is Long and Dreary - Words by Adelaide Anne Procter. Published 1871.
Morn, Happy Morn - Composed for the play, Olivia by W. G. Wills. Published 1878.
The Sisters - Words by Alfred Tennyson. Published 1881.
Wreaths for our Graves - Words by L. F. Massey. Published 1898.
Fair Daffodils - Words by Robert Herrick. Published 1904.

Church Songs
By the Waters of Babylon - Composed c. 1850. Unpublished.
Sing unto the Lord - Composed 1855. Unpublished.
Psalm 103 - Composed 1856. Unpublished.
We have heard with our ears
(i) Dedicated to Sir George Smart and performed at the Chapel Royal, January 1860.
(ii) Dedicated to Rev. Thomas Helmore. 1865.
O Love the Lord - Dedicated to John Goss. 1864.
Te Deum, Jubilate, Kyrie (in D major) 1866.
O God, Thou art Worthy - Composed for the wedding of Adrian Hope, 3 June 1867. Published in 1871.
O Taste and See - Dedicated to Rev. C. H. Haweis. 1867.
Rejoice in the Lord - Composed for the wedding of Rev. R. Brown-Borthwick, 16 April 1868.
Sing, O Heavens - Dedicated to Rev. F. C. Byng. 1869.
I Will Worship - Dedicated to Rev. F. Gore Ouseley. 1871.
Two Choruses adapted from Russian Church Music, 1874.
(i) Turn Thee Again

(ii) Mercy and Truth
I Will Mention Thy Loving-kindness - Dedicated to John Stainer. 1875.
I Will Sing of Thy Power. 1877.
Hearken Unto Me, My People. 1877.
Turn Thy Face. 1878.
Who is Like unto Thee - Dedicated to Walter Parratt. 1883.
I Will Lay Me Down in Peace - Composed 1868. Published only in 1910.

Christmas Carols & Songs

Advent
Hearken unto me, my people - An Anthem for Advent or General Use. Words from Isaiah. (1877)

Christmas Carols
All this night bright angels sing - Words by W. Austin. (1870)
I Sing the Birth - Words by Ben Jonson. (1868)
It Came Upon the Midnight Clear - Words by E. H. Sears.
Part Song for Soprano Solo and Choir (1871)
Hymn Tune "Noel" (1874)
Upon the Snow-clad Earth (1876)
While Shepherds Watched - Words by Nahum Tate (1874)
Hark! What Mean those Holy Voices? - Words by John Cawood (1883)

Songs
Christmas Bells at Sea - Words by Charles Kenney (1875)
Two songs from The Miller and His Man - A Christmas Drawing Room Entertainment. Words by F. C. Burnand (1874)
The Marquis de Mincepie
Care is all Fiddle-dee-dee
The Last Night of the Year - Part Song - Words by H. F. Chorley (1863)

Chamber Music & Solo Piano
Scherzo - Piano Solo, 1857, unpublished.
Capriccio No. 2 - Piano Solo (unfinished), 1857, unpublished.
String Quartet - Performed at Leipzig, May 1859. Published 2000
Romance in G minor - For string quartet, 1859. Published 1964.
Thoughts - Two pieces for piano solo, Published by Cramer, 1862.
An Idyll - For Cello and Piano. Composed in 1865 and Published 1899.
Allegro Risoluto - Piano solo, 1866. Published only in 1974
Berceuse - Based on the theme of Hushed was the Bacon from Cox and Box but with additional material.
Day Dreams - Six pieces for piano solo. 1867
Duo Concertante - Cello and piano. 1868
Twilight - Piano solo. 1868

www.ingramcontent.com/pod-product-compliance
Lightning Source LLC
Chambersburg PA
CBHW060136050426
42448CB00010B/2162